YOU ARE THE POWER

ALSO BY J. KENNEDY SHULTZ

Books
A Legacy of Truth

Audios
Gay and God
Heal Your Self-Esteem
Power: The Practice
Power: The Principle
Power: The Product
Richer Living Through Wisdom and Courage
You Are Too Much

YOU ARE THE POWER

A Guide to Personal Greatness

by

J. Kennedy Shultz

Hay House, Inc.
Carson, CA

YOU ARE THE POWER
by J. Kennedy Shultz
Copyright © 1993 by J. Kennedy Shultz

The author of this book does not dispense medical advice nor prescribe the use of any technique as a form of treatment for physical or medical problems without the advice of a physician, either directly or indirectly. The intent of the author is only to offer information of a general nature to help you in your quest for physical fitness and good health. In the event you use any of the information in this book for yourself, which is your constitutional right, the author and the publisher assume no responsibility for your actions.

Library of Congress Cataloging-in-Publication Data

Shultz, J. Kennedy, 1931–
    You are the power : a guide to personal greatness / by J. Kennedy Shultz.
        p.   cm.
    ISBN 1-56170-074-6 : $12.95
    1. Religious Science International—Doctrines. 2. Spiritual life —Religious Science International. 3. Mental healing. 4. New Thought. I. Title.
BP605.U53S588   1993   93-23932
299'.93—dc20   CIP

Library of Congress Catalog Card No. 93-23932
ISBN: 1-56170-074-6

Internal design by David Butler
Typesetting by Freedmen's Organization, Los Angeles, CA 90004

93 94 95 96 97 98   10 9 8 7 6 5 4 3 2 1
First Printing, August 1993

Published and Distributed in the United States by:

Hay House, Inc.
P.O. Box 6204
Carson, CA 90749-6204

Printed in the United States of America on Recycled Paper

DEDICATION

This book is dedicated to Raymond Charles Barker in celebration of his life, and in thanksgiving for his clear and uncompromising commitment to respect the intelligence within all people, by telling the truth, even on special occasions.

"My words will itch in your ears until you receive them."
—Ralph Waldo Emerson

CONTENTS

PART ONE

POWER—THE PRINCIPLE 1
Our Premise Must Be God   4
Honor Your Desires   7
We Must Have a Perfect God   10
The Focus Must Be You   14
Let's Rewrite the Ten Commandments   17
Mind Your Own Business   22
Our Purpose Must Be Growth   24
Grow in Consciousness First   25
Become a Life Giver   27
You Don't Deserve It Until You Do   27
Live Only with Life-Giving Ideas   29
Develop a Consciousness of Power   30
Nobody Wants to Grow   33
Our Action Must Be Mental   34
Real Virtue is Natural to You   37
Becoming a Powerful Thinker   38
All Creative Action is Mental Action   39
Some Rhetorical Questions for You   41
A New Way to Talk to God   47

PART TWO

POWER—THE PRODUCT 49
The Power of Health   50
  Ideas of Health Have Nothing to Do
    with Disease   51
  The Mind That Heals Itself Heals All Else   52
  ''Change Your Mind and Keep
    It Changed''   57
  Take Absolute Responsibility for
    Your Own Thinking   59
  The Great Reward of Healthy Thinking   61
  The Power of Health is with You Right Now   63

The Power of Wealth   64
  Wealth is an Attitude, Not a Commodity   66
  No Mystery in Getting Money   69
  The Rich Do Get Richer and the Poor
    Do Get Poorer   70
  The Givers and the Takers of the World   72
  Move into the Twenty Per Cent   74
  Practical Actions for Wealth   75

The Power of Love   78
  Love is for the Giving   80
  Everybody Loves a Lover   80
  There is More to Love than Romance   82
  You Are Always Full of Love   84
  The Urge is to Give It   85
  Go Out Each Day and Give It!   87
  Stop Failing at Love   88

The Power of Work   89
  You Are Not Your Job   91
  Get Out of It by Getting Into It   93
  What We Think of Ourselves All Day Long is
    What Counts   93
  Understand the Truth about the Power
    of Work   95
  All Work is Service to Others   96
  You Are Always Self-Employed   97
  False Work Attitudes   98
  We Need to Be of Service to Each Other   99

PART THREE

POWER—THE PRACTICE 101
  The Healing Power Really is Within   106
  Heal the Patient, Not the Disease   107
  You Can Do It Yourself   109
  It Only Takes the Faith You Have   109
  The World Explains Misery as Mystery   110
  We Heal Our Lives by First Healing
    Our Minds   113
  We Must Learn to Affirm Great Value   115
  It's Not All in Your Mind   117
  The Idea Must Come First   118
  Make Good Things Come Naturally   120
  You Will Know When It Happens   122
  Getting with the Creative Process   123
  You Don't "Make It Happen"   125
  Demonstrating a Romantic Relationship   125
  Mental Healing for Physical Disease   128

All Healing is God Healing   130
We Never Heal Disease   131
Spiritual Mind Treatment   132
Assuming Personal Responsibility   133
Spiritual Mind Treatment is Not Magic   135
It Always Works the Way It Always Works   136
Healing Comes as Fast as We Can Accept It   137
How to Do Spiritual Mind Treatment   139
     First Step—Recognition   139
     Second Step—Unification   140
     Third Step—Affirmation   140
     Fourth Step—Denial   141
     Fifth Step—Re-Affirmation   142
     Sixth Step—Praise   142
     Seventh Step—Release   143
If It Perplexes You   144
Go in the Opposite Direction   144
You Can Have What's Yours, Not
     What's Theirs   145
How to Go about It   146
What Else to Do   149
A Spiritual Mind Treatment   151

PART FOUR

POWER—THE PRECEDENT 153
The Prayer of Marcus Aurelius   156
Power through Surrender   157
The Will of God   158
Don't Change God's Mind—Change Yours   160
     ''Everything Harmonizes with Me which is
          Harmonious to Thee, O Universe.''   161

"Nothing for Me is Too Early or Too Late
Which is in Due Time for Thee."   162
"Everything is Fruit to Me
Which Thy Seasons Bring, O Nature."   164
"From Thee Are All Things, In Thee Are All
Things, To Thee Are All Things."   164
The Humble Emperor   164

The 23rd Psalm   166
A Song of Praise   167
What Prayer is Really For   168
"The Lord is My Shepherd; I Shall
Not Want."   169
"He Maketh Me to Lie Down in
Green Pastures."   172
"He Leadeth Me Beside the Still Waters."   173
"He Restoreth My Soul."   174
"He Leadeth Me in the Paths of Righteousness
for His Name's Sake."   174
"Yea, Though I Walk through the Valley of
the Shadow of Death, I Shall Fear No Evil;
for Thou Art with Me."   175
"Thy Rod and Thy Staff, They
Comfort Me."   178
"Thou Preparest a Table Before Me in the
Presence of Mine Enemies; Thou
Annointest My Head with Oil;
My Cup Runneth Over."   179
"Surely Goodness and Mercy Shall Follow Me
All the Days of My Life; and I Will Dwell in
the House of the Lord Forever."   182

The Lord's Prayer   184
  The Prayer's Greatest Significance   185
  The Greatest Problem with The Prayer   186
  God Doesn't Speak English   186
  A Deeper Understanding is Needed   187
    "Our Father"   188
    "Which Art in Heaven"   191
    "Hallowed Be Thy Name"   192
    "Give Us this Day Our Daily Bread"   193
    "And Forgive Us Our Trespasses as We Forgive
      Those Who Trespass Against Us"   194
    "And Lead Us Not into Temptation, But
      Deliver Us from Evil."   195
  The Lord's Prayer Restated   196
  Summing It All Up   196

Afterword   201

FOREWORD

Someone once said that the person looking for a helping hand can always find one attached to his arm. This is bad news for anyone who believes that the help one needs lies far outside oneself. This belief allows a person to look for help from everywhere but within, so that there is no need to change but, instead, one can go on expecting external things to change one's life for the better.

However, this is good news for anyone who is ready to be helped in practical and immediate ways. Because the truth of the matter is that we are never going to get any better until we start to do better with what we have right now.

Another excuse for not doing better with our lives is to tell ourselves that we do not have enough intelligence, wealth, education, or opportunities to parlay into something more. But even though whatever we do have may not seem like much, we always have enough. We always have enough to grow on. And growth is the name of the game. Just as there is no life without growth, there is no wealth without it, no prosperity, no loving, no happy outcomes. Growth multiplies whatever we now have to produce more of the same for a better life.

There is a natural resistance to the challenges of growth in all of us, because growth requires change. This change is, primarily, a change of thought. We must change what we choose to believe, how we choose to feel, the issues we think we ought to address, and the issues we decide to let alone.

Many people choose to believe that they cannot make these choices or even consider the possibility. They do not want to change the way they think because deep down they perceive that with internal changes, external changes will follow and, as a result, they will have to give up many things that they depend on. They think that their entire lives depend on what are actually excuses for past wrongdoing, for avoiding painful corrections, for maintaining relationships that aid and abet their supposed helplessness, and prejudices that let them project their bad feelings onto others.

The old adage that ''when the going gets tough, the tough get going'' applies here. When the sick and tired get sick and tired of being sick and tired, they are ready to take hold of whatever wit and courage they have left and start to make something better out of their lives. They no longer wait for ''something'' to happen to them. They take action.

This is the beginning of certain growth. How far it takes us into better living depends entirely upon our own persistence and not on anything else. Although we do not know where or how far it will take us, we can be certain that until we start changing our thoughts, we are not going to get very far at all.

Absolutely nothing is going to happen *to* us that does not happen *through* us, beginning with our mind and emotions, our thoughts and feelings. It will happen through the way we allow ourselves to think most of the time and through the kinds of feelings that possess us as the result of our thinking.

The United Negro College Fund uses a very effective slogan in its fundraising activities: "A mind is a terrible thing to waste." When we hear this, we nod in instant agreement. The truth of it is gripping. The mind certainly is a terrible thing to waste. However, it is being wasted regularly by most people, even nice, clever, talented people who know how to do many things well, but who do not know how to live as happily and successfully as they might for all their virtue.

Most of the unhappy, unsuccessful, unhealthy people in the world are not bad people. They are not lazy or stupid. They deserve much more than they normally get. Whatever is wrong with them they would gladly fix if they believed that it were possible.

Their false beliefs hinder change. We must know that we are not in trouble by design or by Divine decree. Our troubles and limitations stem from not fully understanding the enormous creative power of our own consciousness. Therefore, we squander our intelligence in dead-end thinking, resentments, resignation, and superstitious nonsense.

This superstitious nonsense sometimes passes for religious piety. But it is quite possible to live in superstition without being religious at all. Superstition is reverence for, or belief in, the supernatural as the source of our experience. It is the belief that our lives are in the hands of a power that exists beyond nature and, therefore, cannot be responsive to our hearts and minds. It suggests that there is no natural, logical way by which we may grow and heal and prosper. On the contrary, it suggests a life that is shrouded in mystery and controlled by some unseen, distant power.

Superstition causes many otherwise intelligent people to abandon commonsense thinking and practical action in the pursuit of their own greater good. They believe that there are limits to what they themselves can do. They feel separated from the Creator by a chasm too deep to understand and too broad to bridge.

This book is offered to those who would like to know better than *this* so that they can live better than *that*. It is for people who are ready to think of themselves, of all other people, and of God, in greater terms. It is for people who find appeal in the idea that God is not an old gentleman living far above, but a Creative Intelligence in which we all live and move and have our being—an Intelligence that lives and moves and has its being through each one of us. This is a concept that will bring power to all people by placing them directly in charge of their own consciousness, and their own thinking-feeling nature in all circumstances, even when problems seem insurmountable.

Emmet Fox, author of the ever-popular classic, *The Sermon on the Mount*, summarized it all by saying that the way to greater living was simply to ''change your mind and keep it changed.''

Ernest Holmes, the founder of the Science of Mind, concluded that behind the creative power of every human mind, is ''a better way to think and a better way to live.'' Through the simple process of making better thinking the prerequisite for living better, we make better things possible in our lives.

Many of us have thought the wrong way for far too long. We have been waiting for something wonderful outside us to suddenly make us grow wiser and feel better. In this book we talk about totally reversing this approach to life. This book is about living on purpose with power. It is about using the power we already have to good purpose. This power is the power of mind. It is the power of Creative Intelligence already with us and forever inseparable from us. It is about changing your life by changing your mind. And it is about keeping your life moving forward by keeping your mind changed and ever-changing.

All of this is more of a challenge than many, perhaps most, people are ready for. But this book *is* for those who are ready, and also for those who *would like to be* ready.

—J. Kennedy Shultz

PART ONE

POWER—THE PRINCIPLE

Power is an appealing concept. Everyone responds to the possibility of power. All are sure that they would be better off in some important way if they had more power. But it is never just a matter of getting power. It is, instead, always a matter of determining how to use it constructively, because power has no value for us unless it works for us reliably and in a way we can understand.

We do not have to know everything about power, but we do have to know how to use it. We do have to be assured that it will work for us because we will never be sure until we see it at work.

For example, electricity is a power that we use in countless ways every day. Although some students of electricity have great theoretical knowledge about it, no one fully understands this power. However, advanced knowledge is not necessary for people to make electricity work in wonderful ways. If the advanced theoretician doesn't turn on the switch in the correct way, the lights won't go on, despite a wealth of expertise. If the ordinary person (by choice) or even the small child (by accident) does turn on the switch the right way, the lights will go on. The power will work for anyone who knows how to put it to work.

The fact that nobody has ever seen electricity is beside the point. We neither question its presence nor its power because we have seen what it can do.

Our consciousness is the electricity of our lives. It is the power that lights up our mind and enlivens our body. It lets us do, make, be, and become whatever it is we choose.

No one has ever seen consciousness. No one has ever seen the action of mind. No one has ever seen the spirit that enlivens every one of us. But we intuitively know that there is a creative power present and operating in the universe and in our lives, just as we know that there is electricity silently existing everywhere. We know there is consciousness in us because we think. And we know that our thought has power because we are always using it to make things happen.

As is the case with electricity in the physical world, thought, in the realm of consciousness, is a creative power that can be used by everyone. It has a definite way of working that can be learned. It works for anyone who takes the time to discover how to use it. Operating as a principle, a law of its own nature, the creative power of mind is always reliable, always working, always producing something. The big question is, "What?"

We need to understand the nature of this principle and how to relate to it in creative ways. We can learn how to turn it on in our lives to enlighten us with wisdom and inspire us with love. We can then have the vision, the courage, and the will to make wonderful things happen through us, to us, and beyond us in our environment.

To live on purpose with power, we must understand that there is a mental principle involved. There is a way to think that will fulfill our purpose and produce the good results that we seek.

In learning how to use this principle, our premise must be God. We must begin by believing that there is a higher power for good at work in this universe. And we must believe that we can rise up to it and actually use it.

In order to perform effective mental or spiritual work, our focus must be on our own minds. We must concentrate as much as possible on what is in our thoughts, in our hearts, and on our lips. We don't need to ignore the world or to neglect other people, but our focus must always be upon ourselves. Our primary responsibility must be ourselves.

We must believe that our purpose is growth—in making all things new, not atoning for the past, not anticipating the future, not explaining our faults or failures. Not analyzing, but synthesizing. The law of life, the principle of power, is a law of growth. It occurs in the present, not in the past, and not in the future.

Our primary action in this adventure of growth must be mental action. Until we know correctly we cannot do right, live well, or become greater than we were.

We do not need to learn what to do or what to think. Instead, we must learn *how* to think in principle and for good purpose. This includes learning a new way to pray, a new way to carry on our mental or spiritual conversation with the God of our understanding.

OUR PREMISE MUST BE GOD

Purposeful thinking is more than creative thinking. All thought is creative. You and I are thinking creatively all the time with or without purpose. Our thought is always creating or making something happen. The question is, are we doing it on purpose? Are we putting the creative power of our thought behind the ideas that we would like to appear in our lives as the things we live with, as the experiences we live through?

We are all creatures of desire—we are always wanting something. And when we get exactly what we want, we want something else. There is no end to our desiring and there is absolutely nothing wrong with this. This is the way we are, and this is exactly the way we were created to be.

Our ongoing desire is what makes it possible for us to continue to grow, to expand, to prosper, and to live. Life is the movement from one experience to another. The desire for this movement is what keeps us alive. We will never be in trouble with our desires if we understand the rightness of them. We must understand that the particular thing we desire at any given time is always something that represents power to us— personal power—the kind of power it takes to live and grow. Whether our desires are high-level visions or low-level cravings, they represent the power that lets us live with integrity and security. This is true whether we want wisdom and wealth, love and health, a better job, a better education, a better reputation, an expensive car, a comfortable home, a hot meal, or a hot time. It makes no difference at all. We seek our desires because we think, rightly or wrongly, that they will bring us to our own personal power, which is the only real power there is. Personal power is power over our own lives, power over our own well-being. Whatever it is we yearn for represents that power—the integrity, the security, and the strength we need to move on in life.

Real power is always personal power. Real power is never power over other people or power over the world. We may think we need that kind of power, but we don't. Our individual well-being does not come from making other people do our bidding. Nor does it come from making the world over in our own image.

Our power, the power that really means something personal to us, comes from knowing how to live healthfully, lovingly, and prosperously in the world just as we find it, no matter what is occurring around us.

The individual who, in the midst of it all, can find a way to think prosperously, lovingly, and healthfully, is the person who has real power. In every age, in every human crisis—depression, war, famine, epidemic —there have been people who prospered, healed, and lived healthfully and lovingly in the midst of it all and through it all. These are the people who had real power. They knew how to live well under all conditions and with all kinds of people.

Real power is the power over our own consciousness, the power over our own thinking, feeling nature, the power over our own mind and emotions. It is an internal power.

Every person has an exclusive right to this power. You have an exclusive and sacred right because, ultimately, you are the only one who must live with the results of how you use it. Since you have to live with the results of its use, it is divinely right that you be entitled to full dominion over it.

If we are going to exercise our right to such power, if we are going to use our minds to think purposefully, to create what we want, we must draw it into the channel of our thinking. In doing this, our premise must be God.

The premise is that there is a universal creative intelligence within us that can and will realize our desires. We must assume that our great desiring for more life comes from this intelligence. And we must assume that all the wisdom to fulfill our desiring nature comes from that same intelligence. We must assume that the creative intelligence that is *urging* us forward will give us the ideas that will *take* us forward. Otherwise, it would not be intelligence at work.

We must also assume that this creator, creative power, this God, if you like, is whole, complete, and perfect. It must contain all the wisdom, all the love, all the good and wonderful characteristics that we can imagine. There must be a source of all good, and it must be God.

Our premise must be God. God must be what we ultimately rely upon for our good. God must be the basis of all our thinking.

If there is going to be anything new in our lives, anything greater, better, or more desirable than what we have now, it must come from something greater, better, and grander than our past experience or our present situation. What we want is not our past or present. Our desire is for something more. Our greater good must come from a different kind of thinking than we have been utilizing so far. The thinking we have been using up till now, no matter how wonderful, can only produce the same old experiences. Our new good must come from a new kind of thinking backed by a creative power that takes these new thoughts and turns them into new things. We must believe that there is a power that can do all that. Otherwise, we will not even bother trying. So, our premise must be God. It takes a belief in God to get us going in the right direction. God must be our starting point and our frame of reference.

HONOR YOUR DESIRES

Since all of our desiring for something more and new and better comes from God, the creative spirit of life, we must learn to honor our desires instead of discounting them. Most people don't honor their desires; they

devalue them and put them aside. They don't know
that their desires come from on high. Instead, they
think that their desires come from down below, from
a sinful, selfish source. But this is far from the truth.

Desires come from God, the only intelligence there
is. So, we need to honor all our desires. If we will
honor them, rather than discounting them or being
ashamed of them, we will find that the creative mind
of God within us will come forward as wisdom. It will
give us everything it takes to find a way to fulfill the
desires we own up to.

If we don't honor our desires, God, being perfect intelligence, isn't going to let us fulfill them. Every time
we turn away from our desires, we are saying, in effect, "I don't want it, I can't handle it; it's too good for
me." And the infinite mind of God, wanting to give
us what we want, says, "Okay, you're right. Let's
move on to something else." Or perhaps, "Let's go
back to same old stuff."

If we will honor our desires, the infinite creative
power from which they came will then enlighten us.
The power will give us a consciousness that sees beyond all obstacles and will give us the courage to get
us moving.

Most people do not believe in God. This includes the
majority of church-goers and the clergy. They do believe in the *existence* of a God, but they do not believe
in God. That is, they do not believe that God is the
only creative power in the universe and that God is all
good. They do not believe that God is both the source

of our desiring and the source of the fulfillment of all our desires. They do not believe that God is always devoted to finding a way to let us live in greater goodness.

Most people believe that God is a diaphanous old gentleman in the sky, looking down upon us, lording his power over us, and holding our sins, mistakes, and miseries against us. They believe that God has some secret plan for us that he will not share with us. They believe that God loves and supports other people, that God loves and supports some people better than others, loves and supports some countries better than others, loves and supports some races, usually theirs, more than others. They believe God favors some forms of worship over others. And they believe that he sends evil into the world to punish, to teach, and to test us for sincerity.

Now, nobody in his or her right mind can really believe in this kind of a God. That is, no one can really give such a God complete love, faith, and also believe that very much good is going to come from such a character. Nobody wants to turn to such a God for the fulfillment of his or her most dear and precious desires.

That is why so few people pray with any belief that their prayers will be answered. And, indeed, without belief, prayers are never answered.

Most people are not certain that they have any right to what they are praying for. They may be praying for health, for continued life, for love, for the ability to pay bills, for a comfortable home, for a good car, for friends, or whatever, but they don't feel that they have any right to what they want because they do not believe in God alone.

They do not believe that God is the source of their desire or that God is all good. They do not believe that there is a wisdom that can fulfill their desires and is always willing to do so.

Not believing in God, they do not seek the help of God except as a last and desperate resort. When everything else has failed and no one else offers any hope, they say, ''Well, it's time to pray.'' Their prayer is not an affirmation of their desire. It is merely their last gasp.

Few people say, ''Well, I decided I wanted this, so I prayed for it.'' Most say, ''I decided what I wanted, so I went here, I went there, I looked here, I looked there, I called this one, I called that one. Time is running out and I don't have it, so I think I'll pray.''

For most people, the premise is not God. Most people are not operating on the assumption that their lives are being supported by a source of all goodness. Most do not understand that God is all-present, all-loving, all-trustworthy, all-powerful, and *all* for them *all* the time. They do not really believe in God! And, therefore, they have very little faith in the fulfillment of their desires.

WE MUST HAVE A PERFECT GOD

These observations are not directed at people who are trying to get away from God. This book is not for people who are angry at God. It is not for people who do not want to believe in God. This book is essentially and fundamentally God-centered in its nature.

Our premise must be God—a God that we *want* to believe in. Because if we don't want to believe in God, we won't. We don't believe in things we don't want to believe in. We don't love things that we are afraid of, nor do we rely on things that we don't trust. We only depend on things that we think are wonderful and trustworthy.

So we must have a believable God. It must be a God that supports the life, the desires, and the ideas that fill our minds and hearts. It must be a God that supports us in Godlike ways of total wisdom, total love, total givingness, and infinite forgivingness in ways that let all the living live well.

There can be no place in our thinking for a God that is negative or destructive for any reason whatsoever. Our God must be a perfect intelligence that hears no evil, sees no evil, speaks no evil, does no evil, and justifies no evil. Our premise must be a God incapable of sending pain, disease, unhappiness, impurity, imbalance, or imperfection of any kind into its own precious creation. A God that destroys its own creation would not be perfect, but merely insane.

Our God must be a perfect intelligence. Any rational human being knows that you cannot make people healthy by giving them disease; you cannot make people good and loving by hurting and torturing them; you cannot make peace by waging war; you cannot bring sanity into the lives of people by teaching them to live in fear and superstition. If we, as mere mortals, have the common sense to know these things, then we can no longer accept a concept of a God that doesn't seem to.

Our premise must be God. It must be a greater God than the world has ever known. We must somehow get ourselves beyond the kind of a God we must lay down our lives for. What we need is a God we are willing and eager to stand up and live with. We must get ourselves beyond a God that preys upon our fears and faults. We must rise up to a concept of a God that supports all of our great and good desires by giving us the wisdom to know how to let them be so.

Ernest Holmes, the great spiritual thinker who gave us the Science of Mind, approached God in this way. He wrote, "There is a power for good in the universe which is greater than you are and you can use it."

If there is a power for good, it can never be a power for evil. If it is truly for good, it is for the good of "good" people and it is also for the good of "bad" people. Unless it is a power of good for everyone, the "good" people will never get any better; the "bad" people will never get good. And, if this were so, this world would have turned inward and destroyed itself eons ago.

Our world is nothing more than a collection of people growing and thriving. It is a living world unfolding through people in ever-evolving ways. If our growth had ceased at some point where we became as good as we were ever going to get, it would have disintegrated. Life will not support anything that is not capable of growth and unfoldment.

So there is a power for good in the universe. And, if it is in the universe, that means it is right here, right now, all the time. The universe is not a place out there in the cosmos. The universe is the total presence of life everywhere.

Now, if this power for good is in the universe, it means that, whoever you are, wherever you go, whatever you do, all the good there is, is with you always. This power for good moves behind your thought and seeks to express itself through your activities. It means that all the good you will ever know already exists with you right now and is poised to do its work through you right now, too.

And, if this power for good is greater than you are, what wonderful news that is! If it is greater than you are, what you are is not what counts. What it is, is what counts! Stop worrying about what you are. That's not what counts because you are going to change if you have any sense. What this power is, is what counts.

Knowledge that there is a power for good greater than we are lifts self-imposed burdens. We don't have to be perfect because God already is! We don't have to know all the answers because God already does! We can give up the impossible struggle to be perfect, blameless, or flawless. You are never going to be blameless or flawless. You are never going to be all of those things that people think they need to be before they can achieve in the world.

You can give up that burden of trying to be perfect.

You can begin to use your full mind, heart, and consciousness to open yourself up to this power that is

God. You can begin to understand it, see it, and rejoice in it as it helps you fulfill your desires, which are surely the desires of its own creative nature.

This is all we need to be doing in this life. We don't have to be perfect; we just have to try to get better all the time. With God's help and our own clarity, we can achieve this.

But our premise must be God. A perfect God. And we must know that the creative power of all life stands behind us, goes before us, and lives within us, all the time, in all our ways.

THE FOCUS MUST BE YOU

We have established that if we wish to draw creative power into purposeful use in our lives, our premise must be God. That is, we must believe there is such a power and that it is available to us.

We want to learn to use this power correctly. God knows what to do and how to do it. We must learn to use this power to play our part in the creative process effectively.

In order to achieve this goal, we must focus on ourselves. We are not created to live for others. We are not created to compel others to live for us. We are not here to make each other's decisions. We are not here to solve each other's problems or heal each other's wounds. This does not mean that we should not honor one another because unless we do that, we dishonor ourselves. This does not mean that we should not help each other as much as humanly possible.

But it does mean that our primary purpose for being alive is to see that we, ourselves, are fully aware, alert, and productive. It is to be certain that we are always growing in order to be in better control of ourselves and of greater value to our environment.

Our strength, our integrity, our security is God-given. It is not earned in the world. We have to find a way to draw it from within ourselves. The only way is by way of our thoughts. It comes from within us, not from beyond us.

People who know how to use their minds to heal their own hearts and to make their own lives work better are the people who are able to love, honor, forgive, and support their fellow human beings. These are the people who have the most to give with respect to health, kindness, and justice. They can afford to be generous because they have so much to give. They have so much to give because they have made so much out of themselves.

Only the wise have wisdom to share. Only the healthy have strength to support. Only the successful have a good example to set. And only the prosperous have the money to spend and the money to spare to do the things in the world that require money.

There are many things that we all desire. We all want more power. Many of us would attend ten power seminars a day if necessary to achieve this end. We all want good health. We all want success in all its many forms. We all want prosperity—being able to do what we want, pay our own way, be independent.

Nobody has ever achieved these good things by

minding anybody's business but their own. Nor do things come to people while they wait for someone else to mind their business, and/or to encourage, inspire, and tell them what to do and how to do it.

The Bible tells us that our salvation is at hand. This means that the power we need is right where we are, and the ability to use it is always in our hands.

If you are serious about using this creative power that we call God, if you want to direct this power that lives for you in your mind and works for you through your thought, if you want this power to work for you in ways that fulfill your desire for a better life, then the focus of your attention must be *you*.

You are the one! You are the one that you need to depend on. You are the one that you need to make your demands upon. You are the one that you need to change, as change is called for. You are the one that you need to love, to honor, to respect, to rely upon, and to listen to before all others.

Before all others, not *instead* of all others. All good living includes treating other people with respect. But in the intelligent living of your life, the focus must be you. In my life, the focus must be me.

We are all individuals, so the way we go about attaining this ideal is always different in detail but identical in principle. It is the making of a personal life that succeeds beautifully in its uniqueness. It is never altering oneself to become part of another, nor living according to anyone else. We want a personal life that succeeds in its own individuality.

All the good that it takes to obtain our goal originates

in our own particular use of consciousness. God's creativity expresses itself through us by action of our individual, personal, private thought. It uses our desires as inspiration and our common sense as guide.

Don't involve yourself in any ideas, teaching, or theology that obstructs or challenges your common sense. Your essential intelligence can be trusted above everything else. This must be so because your own mind is all you have that is entirely yours. There is nothing in this world that cannot be improved upon. There is nothing so perfect that it should be exempt from being challenged, questioned, or reviewed. There is nothing so sacred that it should be allowed to stand forever just because of tradition. Emerson indicated that nothing is at last sacred but the integrity of your own mind. And that means, nothing!

The tendency to make ourselves forever subject to old ideas and beliefs, even ''good'' old ones, is self-defeating and totally self-destructive! As long as we persist in these bad habits, we are not being true to ourselves.

We are each something more, something greater, something better than the greatest idea that was ever thought. Each one of us has the potential for an even greater experience. Each of us is the means by which God comes into this world.

LET'S REWRITE THE TEN COMMANDMENTS

I know that I am not alone in wondering if we, on the brink of the 21st century, have not technologically

outdistanced our spiritual understanding. Has our
scientific reach exceeded our moral grasp? Do you realize that we now have the capacity to kill more people
in five minutes than once could have been wiped out
in a century of protracted worldwide warfare? As
members of the human race, we must have a deeply
imbedded belief that killing people is an acceptable solution to the problems of mankind. How else can we
explain how we've gotten so proficient at it while, at
the same time, we are still stumbling along ineffectu-
ally trying to master some simple and rewarding concepts, such as brotherly or sisterly love or, if you like,
neighborly love, social justice, and common decency?

From the beginnings of our Judeo-Christian civiliza-
tion, one of our basic tenets has been, ''Thou shalt not
kill.'' As far as I know, that commandment has never
been followed by any instructions from on high that
authorize killing as a preferred option under any circumstances.

We did not acquire the notion that killing is an acceptable human option without a lot of authorization.
We have created the moral codes and the religious systems that hold individual life so cheap and validate
even mass destruction. It is with the tolerance of our
race at large that world leaders can say things such as,
''Well, that bomb will only take out a quarter of a mil-
lion people. Let's not worry too much about that one.
It's an acceptable loss—well worth the risk of achieving our overall objective.'' I always wonder what the
''overall objective'' could be and how we have come
to have people in power who so easily talk that way.

Yet, for many centuries, people have been allowing themselves to judge, in their own private hearts at least, which people it is permissible to kill and under what conditions. All according to a moral code of their own fashioning.

Mankind's persistent reach for God, in the form of our ongoing and inexhaustible efforts to achieve greater religious understanding, reveals that in our heart of hearts we know that there is a greater wisdom, a greater power, available to us that shows us the difference between right and wrong and what to do about it. We have always turned to religious creeds or spiritual leaders for guidance and direction in understanding that which is beyond our present understanding, but which we know must be within our reach.

I believe that one of our biggest problems here is that we have been settling for *negative* direction. We have been focusing more on what we must not do, and not nearly enough on what we can do and ought to be insisting upon if we are really looking towards right action. We cannot make our lives or our world better by trying not to do something we have the urge to do, but only by knowing that there is something better to do and that we can find a way to do it.

I invite you to consider a bold idea. Why don't we rewrite the Ten Commandments? We have never obeyed them very well anyhow. Why don't we turn them more into something like a set of positive directions than a set of negative rules that don't seem to have much payoff?

We really do not need the ''shalt nots'' anymore. Most of us know the difference between right and wrong. We don't need anyone to tell us it is wrong to lie, cheat, steal, envy, kill, and all the rest of that stuff. We don't get into trouble because we don't know what not to do; rather, we get confused when we try to think of the good things we can do to make our lives better. In other words, we're just not sure how to go about it.

Instead of just being told not to kill, why not remind ourselves that it is our most divine privilege to honor all life—under all conditions. Why not teach ourselves to put the sanctity of life ahead of all the problems that life presents to us? Why not learn honor and let the life we honor teach us how to live it better?

This concept can be seen as a matter of redirecting the power of our thoughts so that we undergo a conversion of consciousness. Then we can focus on the benefits of patience and right action and how to achieve these aims. In this way, we are turned away from fear of doing wrong, which, of course, often leads us nowhere but right smack into it. For, like it or not, consciousness must create its own experience.

Let's rewrite the Ten Commandments, and let's make new demands upon our religions and our religious leaders at the same time. Let us demand a religion that speaks to us about our essential goodness and power, our right to experience it, our obligation to use it, and the joy that is certain to come from it all. Let us reject any religion that tells us that we are bad, weak, and in need of being warned against the evil of the world and all the misery that evil is going to bring to us. That is not religion. It does not lead us to God. It leads us to meanness and misery.

Let us find a way to learn how to recognize the best of ourselves, which is our God-given intelligence, and how to put it to work to make the best of the world we are sharing. And let's make some very clear, yet positive, rules that remind us how to accomplish this. We will be much more likely to follow such rules because teachings that are based in negativity have very little appeal and are unnecessary when the positive way is clear and inviting.

I am certain that we can make a better world when people, from childhood, learn things such as:

• *Thou shalt honor life wherever you see it, because wherever life is honored, goodness must flow.*

• *Thou shalt respect the property, honor the achievement, and celebrate the happy relationships of all others, because all are wonderful examples of the goodness that is at work in your life, too.*

These commandments appeal to our common sense and our common needs. They are spiritually elevating and practically rewarding. This concept is important because we live in a world that calls for practical results. The goodness we crave must not be put on hold for eternity. We must be able to count on improvement and happiness in the here and now, not merely in the whenever and wherever. Because wherever we are, and whenever it is, we are always living in the eternal here and everlasting now. And the sooner we learn to live with profitable results, the better.

MIND YOUR OWN BUSINESS

We need a new set of rules to establish a new order of thought and a new way of living. And the first of these new commandments should be: *"Mind your own business."*

Through the living of a healthy, prosperous, life the focus of all our mental and emotional activity must be upon ourselves, because the power we need comes from within us, through the action of our thoughts. Therefore, our focus must be on the way in which we are using our minds.

We must focus upon the way we think about ourselves, the way we think for ourselves, and the way we think in the face of all things. We must focus upon the way we think within our hearts, in that private place that nobody knows about but us.

The famous scripture says, "As a man thinketh in his heart, *so is he.*" It does not say, "As a man thinketh in his heart, *so are they.*" As the individual thinks in his heart, so is that individual. The ideas that we create and that we allow to dominate our lives help to create our own experiences before they do anything else, whether they impact anyone else at all.

Even though we may be thinking about others, we are always thinking for ourselves. That is a point we must remember. Our thoughts always do something to *us*. They may or may not influence the person we are thinking about, but they always do something to *us*. They give us their nature: Loving thoughts will always lead us to love; hateful thoughts will always cause negativity to rise up in our lives.

Take care that you are in charge of your thinking. Learn how to make your thinking correspond to your desires. Make certain that your thinking always draws upon ideas that create pretty pictures. Direct your mind to create thoughts that you would like to see materialize as realities in your own experience.

In the creation of a purposeful life, our premise must be God. We must base our belief on the supposition that there is a power for good in the universe that is greater than we are, and we can use it. But to bring this power to bear positively on our lives, the focus must be upon ourselves and the way we think. You are the way life works in your life. I am the way life works in mine. It works for each of us by responding to our heartfelt desires and what we think of them in terms of our right to have them fulfilled in our lives. It works according to our belief in our ability to live with those desires if they are fulfilled.

Many people fail because they want more than they believe they can handle. Rather than risking failure by trying something wonderful, they settle for creating little good at all. For that same reason, many people stop short of accomplishing the goals that they have been pursuing for years. Fearing success, they sabotage it!

Our primary objective must be to clear our consciousness of every kind of negativity and make it as open, loving, free, and receptive to new kinds of good-ness as possible.

We cannot do this while we are preoccupied with what other people are doing, or ought to be doing, or have done. We cannot be absorbed in what other people think of us or what we think of them. In short, we cannot clear our own consciousness while we are, un-der whatever pretext or whatever justification, caught up in minding anyone's business but our own.

Our focus must be inward, toward that which is yet to come. We must not look outward upon the present negativity or backwards into the past. Everything around us is finished and will soon disappear. We must work on what is to come. We must use our minds to invite new and better ideas into our ex-perience, rather than clinging to or fretting over what is old and no longer serviceable.

Whoever you are, whoever you think you are, whoever you hope to be, whatever you appear to be, whatever you are afraid of being, know that in truth you are full of wonder. You live from a heart that is eternally pure. You live from a mind that is infinitely powerful. And the focus of your consciousness must be upon you—the real you, the greater you, the whole you, the wonderful you that is yet to be.

OUR PURPOSE MUST BE GROWTH

Our premise must be God; the focus of our attention must be upon ourselves, and our purpose must be growth. Because only through growth do we live.

Everything that is created grew out of something. Whether it grew out of the seed in the soil or the seed in the womb, it developed by a process of growth. And as it improves and flourishes, it is through a process of growth.

Whatever we accomplish or receive means very little to us unless it is ours by right of consciousness, which means a by-product of our own growth. We can never really possess or enjoy anything that belongs to someone else. What is ours and what remains eternally in service to us is what we have made out of ourselves.

The Law of Life is a Law of Growth. This growth is primarily a growth in consciousness. Our thoughts are the seeds of our experience, and our life grows from the inside out. What occurs in the mind today, occurs as experience tomorrow. So, until it happens inside, it will never happen outside. If we want to flourish among the things around us, we must learn how to flourish with the thing within us.

GROW IN CONSCIOUSNESS FIRST

Our growth must begin with an expansion of consciousness. We must grow up to embrace greater ideas, healthier ideas, ideas that represent a greater goodness. We must grow away from habitual thinking that embraces hurtful ideas, hateful ideas, ideas that seek fulfillment by causing damage or difficulty for anyone, including ourselves.

We don't have to come to the point of never having a bad idea. Bad ideas occur every day; they come and go. Don't worry about them. Let them come, and let them go.

Use the most of your mind to develop thought patterns that move away from patterns of negativity. This is the way to escape those hateful ideas that harm us as well as others. We must escape from ideas such as, "It is right to be punished; it is right to be diseased; it is right to go without." We must free ourselves from ideas that we must be taught by suffering or that we or anyone else deserves evil, for any reason whatsoever.

We know it is natural and entirely appropriate for an infant to demand that its needs be gratified. Nature programs us, as adults, to respond. We cater to our infants to help them grow up, not to keep them infantile forever. We want them to grow to be independent people who no longer think only of themselves and getting their own way. Grown-up people see themselves as something greater than their environment. They realize that they are able to create the security, the integrity, the prosperity that they crave. Through this feat, they create goodness for other people in their lives and in their world. This is how the adult becomes a secure and happy person.

Our sense of value depends on our sense of being valuable to ourselves and others. Which others? The more the merrier! Sad are those who think they mean nothing to nobody, and that no one would notice, care, or miss them if they were gone tomorrow. Many people suspect this about themselves. To increase our sense of value, we must grow in the consciousness of our own essential worth.

BECOME A LIFE GIVER

The Law of Life is a Law of Growth. We grow and expand and flourish as we grow out of a "taking" consciousness into a "giving" consciousness and, thus, become a blessing to all the living, starting with ourselves.

During the creation of this good, rich, healthy life, our purpose must be personal, spiritual growth. Our purpose must be to rise above an obsession with infantile needs, to move beyond the tendency to respond to life with infantile emotion. Understanding that our power is within, we become personally powerful and independently resourceful.

YOU DON'T DESERVE IT UNTIL YOU DO

Many people never get as much good in their lives as they want because they don't believe they deserve it. And they are correct! They don't deserve it because they are waiting for someone else to tell them, to assure them, that they do. But if we don't know our own worth, how can anybody else possibly know it?

We become worthy by developing a consciousness of self-worth. This is a spiritual endeavor. It most assuredly includes developing a larger idea of God and a better understanding of why we are here and what life is really about.

Growing up involves growing wise in the ways of the universe. Many people who do not have this wisdom are still sitting around at age 30, 40, 50, and more, waiting for their parents to love them better. Only then

will they feel deserving of a good life. Or they are waiting for their children to appreciate them more so they
can feel that they did a good job. The truth is, either
they did a good job or they didn't! What other people
think doesn't determine anyone's worth.

The important thing is to do good now, *right now.*
Sitting around, waiting for society to approve of us so
we can feel deserving, is a hopeless game. No matter
how long we hold our breath and stamp our feet with
infantile passion, no matter how long we sit waiting for
approval, we will not experience a greater life until we
grow within ourselves. Not even if the whole world
bows down before us.

Our desire is the only good reason to grow in goodness and worthiness. Our desire is all we need. If we
needed anything more, nature would have supplied it.
We are creatures of desire, born wanting, always wanting, for as long as we live. We must become aware of
the rightness of our desires and use them as an im-
petus for growth and a better life.

There is absolutely no need to seek a greater understanding of this creative power we call God unless we
want to discover how to put it to work in our lives and
change ourselves into something better. If this is our
self-admitted desire, we must first commit ourselves to
learning whatever it is we need to learn. We must become willing to know whatever is necessary to allow
us to change. We must become this way before we
know exactly what will be demanded of us.

Second, we must become willing to change anything, even our most cherished opinions, especially the

ones we have been defending most frequently and fervently over the years. We must become willing to give up whatever we really need to give up, including our most comforting prejudices.

We then become open, receptive, and free to develop a new way to think, a new set of values, a new set of ideas, and a new way of addressing the issues in our lives. Our mind becomes clear enough to let us recognize, accept, celebrate, and use every idea that we believe is life-giving.

LIVE ONLY WITH LIFE-GIVING IDEAS

A life-giving idea is one that gives life to everyone, on all occasions and for no special reason at all. It must be an idea that leads us in ways of thinking, acting, and reacting that express goodness to all and about all, including ourselves and our myriad activities—even the ones we are fond of flagellating ourselves over. At the end of a chain of thoughts moving forward from a life-giving idea, we can come to a conclusion that we can live with.

A life-giving idea permits us to know better than we knew before, to feel better than we felt before, and to do better than we did before. A life-giving idea saves us from being oppressed by everything that is going on around us. It lets us rise above any present condition by letting us see that we are more important than it is. When we greet any desire for our good with a clear "that's for me," we infuse it with vitality.

We become people who can help out in any situation

by giving it the benefit of our goodness. That goodness may amount to no more than the goodness to let it be. To drop it! To let it go! Sometimes that is all the goodness that we can give. Sometimes that is the very best we can manage to do with respect to certain people, events, or things. If this is all we can do, the best we can do, there is no failure, because it is our greatest gift. Life never demands more back from us than we are truly able to give.

Life-giving ideas work well for us and speak well of us as decent human beings. Thinking indecent thoughts and encouraging indecent feelings don't work toward success, only failure. And it doesn't matter if nobody knows we are doing it but us. As they say, you can't fool Mother Nature!

DEVELOP A CONSCIOUSNESS OF POWER

More and more people are waking up to their need to grow. They are actively searching for ways to do it. This is fabulous! Those who are in earnest will find what they are looking for, in spite of themselves. As long as you are earnestly looking, you can't go wrong. Ultimately, you will find it, no matter what. Those who are not earnestly looking, but just going along for the ride, will at least keep out of harm's way for a while. But even the most sincere seekers often labor under a serious handicap because they do not know what they should be looking for. They often waste a lot of time looking for something less than it takes to bring themselves to real power.

Typically, we seek to improve our lives by learning how to make things happen. We hear, "I'm going to go out and learn to succeed, learn how to win friends and influence people, how to get ahead." But we already have a head. The challenge lies in discovering how to use it correctly.

There are certainly ways to make things happen. There are ways to make friends and influence people. There are ways to get ahead. Nothing is wrong with doing any of these things. We can get to the point where we are able to succeed, to win, to achieve, over and over again. But we cannot grow in power until we develop a consciousness where we think of ourselves as power. We can devote ourselves to going out and getting this, going out and getting that. We can even do it with the right attitude. But we cannot grow in power until we develop a consciousness where we think of ourselves as power. We must grow into an understanding that power comes when you go inside, not when you go outside. Without this understanding, none of our achievements will bring a sense of security, a sense of integrity, a sense of easy living. None of it will let us get to the point where we can live a successful life without great stress. None of it will bring about the ability to live without fear and friction.

The scriptures ask the famous question: *What does it profit a man if he gains the whole world and suffers the loss of his own soul?* This does not mean dying and going to hell. This question is about life. It is not a morbid query. This question makes one wonder what good it is if we get ourselves to the point where we're able to get anything we want, but have to struggle too hard, risk too much, suffer too greatly in the process? What good is it if we can't enjoy the fruits of our labors and if we always fear losing it all?

The struggles, the fears, and the suffering come when we don't understand where our good comes from. The Law of Life is not a law of acquisition. It is a Law of Growth. You and I are not created to go out and get anything. We are mandated by life to grow up and become something. And what we want to become is powerful individuals. We want to become people who are always growing in wisdom, who are always growing in love, and who are always growing in the capacity to express it all purposefully and profitably.

This is the consciousness that compels all good things around us to flow into our lives. This is the consciousness that lets us enjoy all good things and use them to please ourselves and bless everyone who looks upon us.

We need to get past the idea that there is any such thing as getting our good at someone else's expense. If it is really good for you, if it is legitimate, if it is of true value, it makes you happy, and it brings happiness to everyone who sees it. It can't possibly do one without the other.

This growth requires effort, and we are up to it. We are built for action. We cannot sit around acting spiritual and doing nothing else. Acting spiritual and waiting for Heaven to rain down its riches doesn't work. But growth can come without undue stress or strain and without exposing ourselves to any great danger.

Of course, growth does not occur without some

problems along the way. The good life is not the life that exists without problems, but many people don't realize this. They don't think they will be successful people until they have no problems whatsoever. Praying for a life that has no problems is like praying for a straight line on your EKG. Life is not supposed to be lived without problems. Problems are the way solutions come about. Problems are the things that get us thinking, that get us stirred up and proactive. We know that on the other side of every problem is its correct answer, and it is always a better idea than we had before. That is exactly what we are looking for.

NOBODY WANTS TO GROW

As the great Goethe observed, *"Everyone wants to be something, but nobody wants to grow."* You may think this doesn't apply to you, but it most certainly does. It also applies to me. It applies to all of us, because none of us really wants to grow. There is something built into us that makes us want to fight growth tooth and nail every step of the way.

If any of us ever do grow, it is because we at last realize that we aren't going to get anywhere until we do. The commitment to growth does not come from an affection for it. It all too often comes out of desperation, and it always comes out of a desire to live better. Finally, we realize that we simply must do it. So at last we do.

If we had our own way, virtually every one of us would have stayed in the womb. We had to be forced out. It is the safest place we have ever been and possibly the safest place we will ever be—in this world, at least. Much of the infantile nonsense we get mixed up in during our lifetime probably comes from a hidden desire to get right back in the womb and stay there.

You see, we do not want to grow. We'd like to stay right where we are even though we can't see much and can't go very far. But it is warm and secure place and we are used to it. We want to remain exactly as we are and have the rest of the world change around us. We want the rest of the world to accommodate us and do for us all those things that, in the long run, only we can do for ourselves. We also want to reserve the right to pass hard judgment on the world when it does not comply with our wishes.

But life will not permit us to stay in one place. Life demands our growth for its own success and for ours as well. This growth comes through using the creative power that surrounds us, fills us, and moves through us. It is the power of our mind. This power follows the direction of our thoughts, letting us grow in wisdom, in love, and in goodness by whatever name, when it is directed to do so. This power compels the world around us to respond to us in kind. This is the way life works. And it works this way for anyone who will work this way with it.

OUR ACTIONS MUST BE MENTAL

We have come to understand that if we can learn to rely upon our mind to serve our well-being, we are at last free. We are free from the need to hope that our well-being will come to us on some far-off day, maybe.

We are free from trying to figure out, without very much information, how to make that hope come true. We are free from worrying about the disposition of someone else to give us our good. And we are free from fearing that we probably won't get much good at all.

Everyone has heard the scripture that says, *"You shall know the truth, and the truth will set you free."* It is one of those very popular Biblical remarks that many have heard, but few have thought out. The truth that it refers to is not the doctrine of any church, nor is it the opinion of any preacher. The truth is that life works to express greater goodness, to express its own good nature in, as, and through all the living. When we know the way life works to provide such goodness, we know the truth. This truth will set us free from all sorts of morbid ideas, morbid emotions, fears, and resentments.

The truth is that the way life works in each individual is through his or her thoughts. Each of us is our own truth, and our own truth is always available to us. Nothing can be more responsive to us than the action of our own thoughts. The real creative power of life, the truth of life, is the action of mind and the power of thought. This is the truth!

So, if we are to come to a place of power and purpose in our lives, our primary objective is to learn how to think correctly. We must learn how to understand the difference between the things we ought to be thinking and the things we have absolutely no business thinking. We must recognize the things that have never brought good into our lives, do not speak well of us, do not speak well of our past, and do not speak well for our future. No matter how emotional or compelling they may be, such ideas are self-defeating and have no business in our thinking.

We must learn the difference between a good idea and a bad idea, and about our right and our responsibility to give our attention to those things that are worth thinking about. This is what we want to learn to do as our natural way of thought. We can't think correctly all the time. As long as we are living in the world where the great ''they say'' impacts our senses, and as long as a single critic survives, we will have our moments of thinking lesser thoughts.

Thought is the essential thing in the living of a well-lived life, so our primary action must be mental. Of course we want to be well-behaved and have good manners. If we don't, we will never get invited anywhere. We want to know how to act right, how to be pleasing and agreeable. We want to have a good personality. That is all well and good. But even though the right things that we do are very important, the way we think is more significant. It is essential. It is what leads us to do the things we do, say the things we say, make the choices we make, react the way we react, and be what we appear to be at any given time.

We are always more than we appear to be. But unless we are working with our minds and improving our thought, it will never show. We will never appear to be more. We will never change from today's person into a better person tomorrow.

If we want to grow, act right, and be able to live in

peace and harmony in our world without the stress of worrying if we are okay, if we want to evolve into a person whose spontaneous behavior can be trusted, by-and-large, to be good, appropriate, and productive; if we want to become a person who acts that way with ease and grace—then our primary concern must be the way we think.

REAL VIRTUE IS NATURAL TO YOU

Emerson noted that in his day a lot was said about a man and his virtue, a person and his good acts and pleasant ways. He said that if you could distinguish too clearly between a person and his virtues, there was not much truth to either one of them, because real goodness and really good actions are not separate from the innate consciousness of the individual. Actions that do not spring spontaneously from good thoughts are not virtues. They are merely good manners.

Now, there is nothing wrong with good manners. However, the only way that we can act with genuine value and the only way we can get the world to react to us with genuine empathy is by the right action of our mind when we habitually and spontaneously think the right way, even when nobody is watching, even when nobody really expects anything of us, and even when we are not on the hot seat.

When we think the right way, whatever we are doing and with whomever we are dealing, our actions tend to be correct. They tend to contribute, to improve the situation or, at least, not make it worse.

Many times the only thing we can do when we don't know what to do is to have the wisdom to do nothing. And when we don't know what to say, we should have the good grace to say nothing. There is not anything wrong with simply shutting up sometimes. Be willing to bite your tongue in half rather than put down yourself, someone else, life, or the situation. If you cannot make a positive, loving comment, say absolutely nothing.

We look for correct actions and correct reactions. Then, whatever comes out of our mind and, thus, our mouth, works in some way to contribute to the healing of that situation. At least it does not make it worse. A consciousness committed to right thinking and dominated by right attitudes will always lead to right conduct. It may not do it instantaneously, but it will do it before tragedy occurs. It will do it sooner than later. And then we will never again have to say to ourselves, ''You were too late. It's too bad. You should've thought of that sooner.''

BECOMING A POWERFUL THINKER

So this is the consciousness that heals. It is the consciousness that makes a person powerful. Truly powerful! It turns us into powerful thinkers as we address the ups and downs of everyday life. It turns us into powerful thinkers while addressing the baffling things in life. We now bring power into the midst of great adversity!

This is a consciousness that is filled with more clarity than nonsense. It is consciousness that is filled with more courage than fear, and more wisdom than ignorance. It is a consciousness that is far more impressed by its own wisdom and its own competency than it will ever be confused and dismayed by all the terrible things happening in the world.

Developing this consciousness is the best way to achieve personal healing in our lives. Nothing can get better until we do. We are the thinker behind the appearance, the healer of our lives.

ALL CREATIVE ACTION IS MENTAL ACTION

Through the creation of this type of consciousness, the action—the primary action—must be mental. Therefore, we must be more concerned with thought than with appearances. We must become more devoted to correcting what is going on inside us than with changing what is happening on the outside.

We cannot create a better life merely by acting as we think we ought to. Everybody knows how to act as they think they ought to. If we didn't, we'd all be in jail. But pretending that things are great when they aren't is self-delusion. Pretending to like what we really dislike, just to impress people, is self-betrayal. So is acting as if we believe or care about things that really don't make any sense to us. All this false acting is an insult to our intelligence and a deterrent to our learning ability.

Many people do things to get others to treat them right. Of course, it is very natural for us to want to live in a world where other people do right by us. However, if that is our first concern, it must be because we think that they are not naturally inclined to treat us well. And this has to mean that we think there is something wrong with us, or them, or life, or God, and that we are living in a situation that is basically hostile.

We know bad things happen to good people. Some of the dearest people we will ever meet suffer terribly in life. Some of them suffer their entire lives. But it is not because they do not know how to act good; they do. It is because they do not know how to think right!

Everybody says, "Oh, what a good person. Why is she so bad off?" It is not because God does not love her or because life is unwilling to reward her for acts of goodness. Rather, it is because she and many others like her lack a big enough concept of God. They lack a great enough belief in the goodness of life. And they certainly do not have a good enough opinion of themselves.

One of the greatest things that I was ever taught was: *"Never, never, never criticize yourself."* We never need to. There are always other people to do it for us—our relatives, our neighbors, our co-workers. We need to develop a good opinion of ourselves, not tear ourselves down.

Many good people don't know how to think right about themselves and about God. They don't have a big enough idea about the goodness and purpose of life. They don't think that they are good enough to deserve all the good that is around them, all the good that so many others are getting. These good people are not letting themselves become wise enough to make better choices. They are not letting themselves become loving enough to be able to approve of themselves and to think of themselves kindly.

SOME RHETORICAL QUESTIONS FOR YOU

Consider these rhetorical questions in the privacy of your own mind. Decide their significance in your life.

Do you really think of yourself kindly?

Do you really think of yourself as the kind of individual who deserves the very best out of life? And if not, what good is that doing you or anyone else, including God?

How is life on any level, on earth or in Heaven, being improved because you do not think kindly of yourself, and because you are not making yourself available for the greatest amount of good possible?

What good is it doing you or anyone else if you don't use the full power of your own limitless thoughts to stop thinking of reasons why you shouldn't have the best of everything?

What good is it doing you or anyone else if you don't spend your time forming a concept about life and God and yourself that involves life being good to you, God being fulfilled through you, and you being happy?

When you finish with those rhetorical questions, here are some more:

Do you think it is a sign of virtue to be ravaged by some disease? Do you think that it makes you better than you were

before? Do you think it's going to make you morally or
spiritually better than you otherwise could be?

Do you think that you are earning your way to Heaven by
living patiently in Hell? Do you think anyone in this world
is rich because you are poor, happy because you are sad, or
successful because you are failing? Do you think any of that?

All of that is insane thinking!

To the extent that we remain sick or poor or afraid
or unhappy or limited in any way, we may be certain
that there are concepts like the above that need replacing. There is important mental work to be done, which
can only be done by each unto himself.

If we are going to change any negative things in our
lives, the mental work must be done first, and it must
be done by us. All the creative action that underlies
this negative stuff we have been talking about is mental action; so, all change for the better will come from
a change of mental action.

Nothing happens until somebody gets a new idea
and learns how to believe in it—and believes in it in
spite of everything. In spite of being thought crazy by
others. In spite of whatever misery we fear we must
endure. And in spite of not being sure that we really
believe in what we are trying to accomplish.

Many people are aware that there is something
deeply wrong inside of them. They know that it needs
to be fixed. And many of these people know that
whatever is wrong inside them can't be fixed by any
of the methods that they once thought could do it.

For example, it can't be fixed by going to church. There are people who have been going to church every Sunday and Wednesday for years and are still as confused and unhappy as when they started. Merely going to church won't do it.

It can't be fixed by getting married. Marriage is the great fixer in many people's minds. "It will all clear up when I get married." Today, more and more people know that that simply is not so.

It can't be fixed by moving to another city. This is another popular idea abetted by ever-easier long-distance travel. It can't be fixed by divorce or by quitting the job either.

And it can't be fixed by going back to school. A lot of 40 year-olds who do not know how to live think that returning to college will teach them. When asked, "What are you going to study?" they reply, "I don't know. I'm just going to go back to school." No thought goes into it at all!

So, more and more people are beginning to understand that what needs fixing will not be changed by all those things we once thought or were told would do it. In their misery, they try new and different things. They get involved with more exotic religions, more off-beat friends, untraditional lifestyles, and, perhaps, in occult studies and practices or in unusual hobbies.

Oh, sure, hobbies are a *great* solution! While complaining and moaning and groaning, have you ever been told, "Ah, George, you need a hobby. You need to go out there and find something that really interests you.'' Well, these well-meaning people do not know what they are talking about. What they are really saying to you is, ''You need to find something to do so you won't bore *me* with this stuff.''

It is easy to merely substitute new things that won't work for old things that didn't work. We can easily get involved with everything in the world except our own thought. But we must change our minds to change our lives, and our starting point must be our thoughts. We evolve in power after we get involved with power. And the greatest power available to us as individuals is the power of our own minds, the power of our own thoughts. In the creation of a personal life worth living, the action—the essential action—must be mental.

Remember, all thought is creative, even goofy thought.

All thought is creative because all thought has its impact upon mind. We are always thinking. We are always creating. We can stop doing anything else, but we can't stop thinking. So, what we are thinking about all the time is extremely important.

People, as a rule, don't even have a glimmer of understanding about how they think 24 hours a day. They have never paid attention to their thoughts. They never knew that what they thought mattered as long as nobody else knew. For years they have let their minds get away with murder. With murder! Killing off all kinds of good ideas, all kinds of growth. Killing off all kinds of personal visions of beauty, of excellence, of love.

Since all thought is creative, and we are thinking all

the time, we must make a commitment to watch what we allow in our minds as vigilantly as we watch what comes out of our mouths when we think someone important is near. The truth is, someone important is always near, and it is ourselves. We are our own most important audience.

We have to get in the habit of refusing to think anything that leads to hateful conclusions about ourselves, anybody else, or life in general. We have to impose a discipline on our thoughts that cuts off, as early as possible, any line of thinking that heads in a negative direction about anyone, even if he or she "deserves it." Perhaps, especially, if he or she "deserves it."

We need to get into the habit of telling ourselves that there is a better way to think, even if we, at the moment, don't know what it is. We also need to get into the habit of telling ourselves that every story has a good and perfect ending, even if we, at the moment, can't see what it is. And, having admitted that, we have to shift our thoughts resolutely to something really worth thinking about.

Now, this is really getting involved with power in a creative way. It is taking charge of our minds. It is also taking charge of our lives. Nobody else can do that for us. Don't expect the world to be helpful. Don't even expect the world to understand what you're doing. If what we are doing were common knowledge, it wouldn't have taken us so long to learn about it.

We live in a world that thrives on bad information. It is a world that is endlessly transmitting information to itself, most of which is negative, and much of which is downright morbid. Whatever people are saying has a better possible conclusion than they tend to admit. Don't believe any of their talk. Don't repeat it and don't quarrel over it. It's none of your business. Find a way to respond politely, without buying into it.

When even nice people bombard you with tales of impending nuclear destruction, of how bad the weather is and how much worse it's going to get when the polar ice cap melts, of how there will be new taxes this year no matter what the President says, and of the wicked ways of the world, you can be certain that these people are not the ones who are ever going to fix anything. They are not the ones who are ever going to do anything about it.

Stop listening to stuff like this. When confronted with such negativity, and we all will be as long as we live, there are conventional responses that deflect such comments in a delightful way. The responses I'm referring to are pleasant but meaningless. So they are excellent for this negative kind of input, because it, too, is meaningless.

For example, when you are confronted by such negativity, it is sufficient to say things like, ''Is that so?'' That response is surprisingly effective. ''How interesting.'' Whoever is speaking will almost always lighten up if told they're interesting. ''You don't say,'' is another one. And, of course, ''Thank you for sharing.'' Then, turning within to the privacy of our own minds, we can say to ourselves, ''It's a total lie. There's not a word of truth in it. It's got nothing to do with my life at all.'' Then we can go on our way, and get on with ideas that have value. Through the living of a productive life and the creation of a life of ever-growing goodness, actions must be mental. Until we are fully in charge of the action of our own minds—our thoughts—we aren't in charge of anything.

A NEW WAY TO TALK TO GOD

In addition to the day-to-day mental housekeeping we've been talking about, we need to discover something else. We need to discover a new way to pray, a new way to talk to God. We need a new way to speak to whatever power abounds in our universe.

The Scriptures have told us, when we pray, to pray believing and it will be done. But most people are not trained to pray believing; we are trained to pray not believing! We are trained to pray not believing that it can be done, not believing that it necessarily should be done, and not believing that it's going to be done—at least not for us.

If we pray, we typically think we have to ask for something, beg for something, plead for something. This indicates an idea of a God that is unwilling to give us our good and might not think we deserve it. As a result, when we pray that way, we may or may not get it. And probably not! Since most of what has occured in our past hasn't been what we prayed for, we believe that our prayers will continue to be unanswered. Because, after all, it is done unto us as we believe.

When we pray, if we think we must promise God

something, like giving up salt water taffy or sex, or suffering in some way to show God how deserving we are, we must think of God as avaricious or foolish or sadistic. We can't trust someone like that! So, we cannot pray believing!

But if we can bring ourselves to the point where we think well enough of ourselves, believe enough in ourselves, and in life, and in God, so that we can stand face to face with the universe and know that all the good we seek is at hand, we will have a consciousness that easily fulfills our desires.

If we can announce that we are open, receptive and entirely worthy of our good, if we can proclaim with growing faith that we expect our good, our good will come forth. Because that is the consciousness that heals, blesses, and prospers all of life.

This takes practice. But we're always practicing something, so why not practice this? God wants us all to live well, and there is a way for everyone of us to do just that. Whoever you are, it is always within your reach, because your good really is at hand.

PART TWO

POWER—THE PRODUCT

In Part One of this book we talked about the power of your mind, how it works to create your experience, and how to let it create the things you want in your life. We looked upon Power as the Creative Principle guiding our thoughts.

All creative thought must produce something that has the same nature as itself, as the idea behind it. The power that creates as principle creates only power. But it is power operating in more tangible, visible, and practical ways. It is the Universal Principle coming into being through individual thought. In Part Two, we will see that there is not Principle *and* what it creates. There is only Principle *as* what it creates. Creative power must create something, and in our lives, through our individual thought, it creates many, many things. These things may be grouped into four categories. Knowing how to use the creative power of our minds to produce ease and abundance in each of these four areas is essential for a well-balanced, harmonious, and productive life. These four areas are: *health, wealth, love,* and *work.* They are like four corners of a good foundation. Each corner must be solidly established if the foundation is to be stable enough to support a life worth living. If the foundation is weak in any part, whatever we build upon it is shaky in all its parts. We are interested in wholeness. We desire a well-balanced life. We want to establish strength and depth in all four areas. In health. In wealth. In love. And in work.

Let's begin by realizing that the power of life, in your life, as your thought, is the power of health. It is also the power of wealth, the power of love, and the power of work. Each of these things is creative power expressing life. When we talk about health, wealth, love, or work, we are talking about energy, before commodity. Each is something in mind before it is something in actual experience.

Of course, there really is only one power, the creative power of mind. This power creates the "facts" of your life following the direction of your thought. What we think about the four areas of our life is the power that creates the way we experience each of them. So, without moving away from our basic premise that there is only one power, we can refer to that power as the power of our health, our wealth, our love, and our work.

THE POWER OF HEALTH

As we learn how to experience a full measure of health, let's begin with the idea that all disease is primarily mental. It is mental in origin. Health is the power that eliminates disease by replacing ideas of sickness with better and greater ideas, with life-affirming ideas, with ideas of personal wholeness. The power of health is not the kind of thinking that believes in fighting disease, fearing disease, resenting it, or justifying it. It's not that kind of thought at all. The power of health is the kind of thought that does not believe in disease. It doesn't ignore the fact that there is disease. It just doesn't *believe* in it.

Ideas of health—that is, ideas that create a consciousness of health and thus an experience of health, never include a belief in disease as a power or as a necessity. They do not view disease as something that must happen or as something that serves any purpose whatsoever. Healthy thinking never regards disease as something that is sent to punish us or to teach us. Healthy thinking does not view disease as something that must "run in our family," come to us at a certain age, or occur because of our gender, our physical type, our lifestyle, or any other earthly reason.

IDEAS OF HEALTH HAVE
NOTHING TO DO WITH DISEASE

A consciousness of health is the power that heals. It spends little time thinking about disease or about any excuses for disease, any explanation of disease, any running commentary upon disease. A consciousness of health is never interested in fighting anything. It never has to flee from anything. A consciousness of health is entirely focused upon knowing one thing— that health, wholeness of body and being, is our natural state.

Health *is* our natural state. It is supported in us by all nature, by all God, by all power, by all that is real and true and lasting and holy. All life supports us every time we use our minds to let the power of life, the power we like to call God, the power that creates us all, become the power that governs our health.

To become healthy-minded, we must learn to think this way about health. In this manner, we approach life with a mind at ease. And a mind at ease with itself and the world we live in is a consciousness not prone to disease. It is a consciousness of health. We can put our minds in a state of ease by accepting and believing only in ideas of ourselves as whole, as precious, as worthy of our wholeness, and as grateful for our wholeness. These are healthy ideas. These are the only kinds of ideas that can provide health. And they will always produce health in the life of anyone whose consciousness is filled with, and dominated by, them. These ideas cannot come into our minds unless we put them there, and they will not dominate our thinking unless we make a conscious commitment to think, talk, and act in ways that support them.

THE MIND THAT HEALS ITSELF
HEALS ALL ELSE

The mind that is at ease with life is the mind that heals all else. It is the mind that supports the body in its return to strength and purity and wholeness. There can be no disease where there is no mind to believe in it by fearing it, fighting it, explaining it, justifying it, or becoming obsessed with it. The mind that heals is the mind that is trained to reject all that kind of thinking and does so, no matter what. It does so in the face of all kinds of pain, all kinds of symptoms, and all kinds of opinion, including expert opinion. The mind that is unafraid to think in a way that is contrary to what the whole world tends to believe about health and disease is the mind that heals. This is not a matter of denial of the presence of the disease. It is a matter of affirming the rightness of a life free of it—above it and beyond it—a life of ease for ourselves in the face of it.

The world has always doted upon disease. It has made a dramatic case for it and has studied ways of relating to disease that are very respectable and sometimes even passed off as spiritual. Theology gives sanctified explanations for the necessity of disease. A whole structure exists that teaches how to relate to diseased people as helpless victims from sickness to death. It even encompasses the proper platitudes to say afterwards, "I don't know why the poor soul had to suffer so, but God has his reasons."

The world has always been obsessed with disease, believed in it, prepared for it, expected it and has, in a strange way, come to make it part of its system of worship. The world has always accepted disease as a necessary and natural part of life, as God's way of punishing sinners, as God's way of teaching us a lesson, and, ultimately, as God's way of killing us off to make room for those to come.

The truth is, disease is not God's way of doing anything. Disease is not necessary to life and is not natural in any way. Disease has no purpose, no place, and no real power. It is *nothing* trying to become *something* through a mind that does not know the truth.

Remember, all disease is primarily mental. This does not mean, "It is all in your mind." It most certainly is not "all in your mind." People who say that to sick people are being thoughtless and cruel. And what's more, they are wrong! Disease can most definitely make a very substantial appearance in the body, causing great physical difficulty, and requiring medical care and treatment.

However, all disease starts in the mind. It begins as a false idea about life, about the universe, about God, or about something intimately to do with ourselves. So, if the body is to be truly and finally healed, and if the individual is to be restored to a natural, ongoing state of health, there must be a healing of the mind. There must be the creation of a greater consciousness of health for and about the individual who is suffering from the disease.

Some people go through their entire lives moving from one ailment to another and each ailment is cured on the physical plane. They take one medicine to adjust this, and another to adjust that. At age 52 they get something cut out. At age 56 they get something else patched up or straightened out. At age 62 they go again for more treatment. Finally, they take multiple medications to keep themselves in one piece—if possible. Although they think they are staying healthy, they most definitely are not. They haven't been healthy for years. Eventually, they get some ailment that cannot be straightened out. Then they die, usually much too slowly.

Now, the truth is, years earlier they could have become really healthy. They should have because they could have. But they did not understand the nature of health.

I am not talking about health as getting over one ailment in order to get another one. Instead, I am talking about bringing your life to the point where you are living day by day, year after year, with a minimum of any kind of difficulty that causes you pain, limitation, or impairment in your joy of living. This is true health. Health is not the absence of disease; health is the presence of something natural.

Here is something else that may keep us from getting distracted with silliness. When I say that all disease begins with an idea, I am not saying that one single sick thought will cause us to acquire some horrendous disease. Nor am I saying that an occasional beautiful idea will heal us when we have a terrible disease. Random thought plays very little part in forming the content or the direction of your consciousness. There is no need to be fearful of every negative thought that pops into your head. On the other hand, there is no reason to be optimistic as a result of those sporadic uplifting thoughts that go through your mind. Either way, there is very little impact.

Although our brains are very fragile, our minds are not. Mind is influenced by every thought and feeling to some degree but, on the whole, it is quite resistant

to any real or permanent change in its habitual patterns and direction of thought. Your brain is fragile,
but your mind is as tough as shoe leather.

So, if you are going to commit yourself to healing
your life by changing your mind—that is, by changing
your thought, it is important to understand that this
requires more than occasional good effort. This is more
than "holding a good thought" when the occasion demands. This is more than trying to make things better
by pretending nothing is wrong. It is more than trying
to dismiss difficulties by saying, "It's all in your
mind." It's much more than that.

If you are going to get involved in the healing of your
life by the healing of your mind, get ready to get tough
with yourself in a way that no one else can. Get ready
to get tough with your mind. Get ready to insist and
persist. Insist on moving your mind away from its
traditional tendency to focus on what's wrong, to
worry about what's wrong, and to be overly involved
in thoughts and conversation relating to what's wrong.
Persist in keeping your mind moved away from all that
kind of thinking even when all the world wants you
to do otherwise.

You know, when people ask you how you are, they
hope it's bad. It's sad but true! People look for bad
news. They don't want to hear, "I'm on top of the
world, I've got lots of money in the bank, and everyone loves me." If you say that, they'll never speak to
you again. When they say, "How are you?" they are
inviting you to draw close to them by telling them how
much misery you have. We live in a world that loves

misery. And if your primary idea is to be in "right relationship" with the world by agreeing with it, you're dead. Your primary idea needs to be in "right relationship" to the universe, to God, to nature, to the power that heals. That's where your life comes from, and that's where your healing comes from, too.

"CHANGE YOUR MIND AND KEEP IT CHANGED"

Emmett Fox, when asked, "What can I do to heal myself of all this trouble?" said that when you get through with all the lectures and all the reading, when you get to rock-bottom, when you're really ready to *do* it, what you have to do is, *"Change your mind and keep it changed."*

Ernest Holmes put it another way. He said, *"Don't look at the problem; look at the solution."* This is hard to do because the problem is always glaring, and the solution often seems vague and distant, and not terribly compelling. We must look inward toward what will work for us when the world doesn't have the answers we need or the heart to give us the kind of encouragement we long for.

By nature, mind does not change easily. If it did, we'd be in a state of confusion most of the time. Mind does not change every time a new idea flies by. We wouldn't be able to survive one day of television if it did. Television would be banned, outlawed, because it would make us even crazier than it already does!

But, by nature, mind must change if we want to

change our outer experience. So, in order to change that which does not change easily, we must get tough with our minds. Our minds can stand it. They are not fragile. Insist and persist, and do it all without fear. Do it all without anger.

You see, it can be done without fear or anger when we understand that we will win. We can trust in winning through insistence and persistence because we can trust in the nature of mind. The forward movement of life is possible only as mind changes. When we really understand that mind must change, we can be tough. We can be forthright without doing a bad number on ourselves. We don't have to be negative, cruel, and impatient with ourselves. We know that mind can change, will change, and eventually must change as life continues. So, we can get serious about changing it our way, and now. We do not take its natural resistance to change as our failure. We cannot fail if we persist. There is no failure in the mind of God, and there need be no failure in our minds either.

We need to get tough and take charge of our thinking and direct it where we want it to go. We must focus it on the kinds of ideas we want it to duplicate. If we do not work with our thinking in this way, mind will work against us. In other words, it will go right on working the same way that caused the problem in the first place.

We must understand that the power of mind is both the power that binds us and the power that can just as easily set us free. This is what Ernest Holmes meant when he told us, *"The thing that makes you sick is the thing that makes you well.''* That ''thing'' is mind and the way we use it. When we're in trouble, we don't have to go looking to see what to do about it. We simply take what got us into trouble—our mind—and use it in a different way. Mind will get us out just as it got us in. It must because that's the way it works.

TAKE ABSOLUTE RESPONSIBILITY FOR YOUR OWN THINKING

Whether we are interested in spiritual healing because we are sick and have little hope of recovery by ordinary means, or because we are tired of living in fear of getting sick, or simply because we are dismayed by the prospect of having to end our days on the planet with some stupid illness, the message is always the same: *The way to use the power of mind as the power of health is to take absolute responsibility for changing our own thinking.* We can do this whether or not there is a good teacher around to help us, whether or not there are people in our lives that agree with us, whether or not we can find the right inspirational literature. We can do this, no matter what!

We can take absolute charge of our own thinking and create a consciousness dominated by healthy ideas. We can do this in spite of what the world around us says we ought to believe or ought to expect. No one can put us in charge of our thoughts except ourselves. And no one can block our access to our own creative thinking.

Of course, this is easier to do before we are sick.

However, it is possible regardless of how sick we are. Someone may wonder, ''Do I have enough time left to heal myself of this awful disease before it kills me?'' When they say this and look at me with hopeful eyes, I always have to say, ''I have no idea.'' Because I don't. But I do know that if you don't try, there's no possibility at all. I also know this—that a life spent reaching for something better, whether it is a long life or a short life, will be a better life than one spent struggling with disease, living in pain and outrage and limitation, expecting little good.

The purpose of our life on this planet is not to avoid death. That's big news to a lot of people. They think that is why they're born, to keep on living. They do the most extraordinary things because someone says it might keep them alive a little longer. But trying to avoid death is a hopeless idea because death is natural; it is not to be avoided. Disease is unnatural; it is not to be endured. Death and disease have no real relationship. We don't have to get sick to die. Most people do not know this. They're tired of living, but they don't know how to get off of this planet. So they invent an illness, bring it upon themselves, burden themselves and everybody else with it for years, then finally die.

No! Avoiding death is not the purpose of life. The purpose of life is to live in freedom and joy and ease until death moves us on to whatever comes next.

There are many, many people who live wholesome, healthy, active, and abundant lives. Then one day, after they've done what they needed to do, at a time known only to their inner selves, they sit down to read the newspaper and go right off. Or perhaps they go to bed and don't wake up. Upon such an occurence, everybody says, "Oh, poor Lucille." What do they mean, "Poor Lucille"? She's better off than you are. And may well have had better sense. Don't mourn Lucille. Consider her a good example.

I'm often reminded of the story of the 96 year-old lady up in the mountains of Tennessee who finally died. When they all gathered for the funeral, the very sophisticated cousin from Atlanta came along weepily and said, "Oh, poor Granny, what did she die of?" And the country cousins just looked at him. They didn't know what to say. "What did she die of?" the city slicker repeated. Finally, someone answered, "She died of a Tuesday!"

We don't have to die of anything. Death and disease have no real relationship at all. The fact that so many people get sick before they die means that they don't know how to live well, so they don't know how to die well either.

THE GREAT REWARD OF HEALTHY THINKING

The great reward in this life for creating a consciousness dominated by the power of health is that we cease to fear death. And when we do not have a morbid fear of death, the good life really begins. Only then can we go out and think as we want to think and do as we want to do without fear of being struck down and taken away to some dreadful eternity.

When Jesus talked about overcoming death, he was

not talking about avoiding the physical act of dying. He experienced the process of physical death himself, showing no fear of losing life. There are many who believe that he is coming back someday, but I rather doubt this because, while life certainly is eternal, it is not repetitive. There is a way for it to continue without resurrecting the same form, the same personality, and identical objectives. You may subscribe to the reincarnation theory and believe we all come back into human form in this world, or you may believe there are other forms, not of this world, through which we may be endlessly recreated. Either way, life is an eternal experience. And either way, life remains entirely creative because it remains an entirely originating experience. Repetition is not the action of an unlimited creative power. Repetition is what people do when they don't know what to do next. Jesus does not have to come back as Jesus to take his message further. The creative intelligence in, as, and through all, is perfectly capable of doing that, and is doing it wherever there is receptivity to it.

When Jesus spoke of overcoming death, he was talking about the fear of death, not the fact of it. When this fear has been conquered, we are able to live with what Ralph Waldo Emerson called ''immeasurable mind.'' This is a mind unafraid to think boldly, to think clearly, to explore deeply, to seek healthful ideas on its own behalf. It is a consciousness that does not need to search for support and encouragement outside of itself. It does not need to bow to the beliefs and expectations and fears of the world in order to be all right.

If you can disconnect the ideas of death and disease, and realize that one is not a necessary prelude to the other, you can proceed to the understanding that disease is not natural, has no power, and does not belong in your life for any reason. The mind that comes to this understanding, releasing all fearful belief about disease, is the mind that can do precise mental work, get healthy through and through, and stay healthy in a world that believes we must all get sick. Once we understand that our real nature is health, all power moves into our lives to support that understanding. It creates for us in our outer experience what we know as the truth inside. Health of body is the great reward of healthy thinking.

THE POWER OF HEALTH
IS WITH YOU RIGHT NOW

I do not believe that people get sick simply because some sickness runs in their family, or because a germ or virus or some other bug gets into their bodies and sets up camp. There is and always has been all manner of disease running through families. But there have always been people in those families who never got a touch of it. There are and always have been and always will be bugs living and dying in bodies, with new strains being developed every split second. This has always been the case.

I believe that we get sick because we are conditioned to believe in sickness as necessary, as deserved, as instructional, as a part of life, and as necessary for death.

We have a field of expectation that believes in disease and creates it. I believe we stay sick because we think illness is more powerful than health. And I believe the way to become healthy is to change our minds, our beliefs, and our views of the meaning of life and death. The only way we can do this is to become personally responsible to ourselves for finding a way of thought that makes sense to us. We must get tough with ourselves about what we're going to believe and what we're not going to believe. Then, as we open ourselves to this kind of healthy thinking, all power becomes a power of health in our lives. It does its healing work in every part of our body. Such is the power of health, and whoever we are, we have it with us right now.

THE POWER OF WEALTH

Now we come to the power of life as the power of wealth. Real wealth is represented by the good things that we can produce in our lives as the direct result of what we have created in our minds. Let's look into the business of how to think creatively in order to produce purposefully. We can learn to be the types of people who are not always looking around wondering how or why something happened to us. When we don't know how it happened, we can't know how to make it happen again, if it was good, or how to keep it from happening again, if it wasn't. It is very important to know how to make it come again or how to avoid it. This is purposeful thinking. It is positive and creative thinking.

Since we are created as individuals, each one of us wants very different things in our lives. But because we share the same life and because we are served by the same creative intelligence, all of our particular desires have something in common. For one thing, they fall into the same categories. Whatever it is we want, whatever it is we feel we are lacking, falls into the categories of health, or wealth, or love, or good satisfying work. We all want to live lives in which we have a body that is healthy, that moves with ease and without pain, and does what we want it to do. We all want the ability to live freely, to get what we want, to spend what we want, to live where we want, and to do what we want. That's wealth! We all want relationships that are marked by love, decency, and proper regard, in one way or another. And we all want to live a life in which whatever work we are doing, whether it is out in the world or at home with our families, is work that is well done. We want it to be work that lets us feel that we are meaningful, not only to ourselves but also to the people who look to us for meaning. That is the world of work. A worthwhile life depends upon knowing how to demonstrate success and stability in each area. So, our desire for wealth or prosperous living is a natural desire and one that we have every right to fulfill. There is nothing mean or selfish about it. It should never be denied. And the possibility for our prosperity should never be doubted.

We must begin by understanding a very important point: Wealth is something much, much more than money. It is something that must come into our life before any amount of money can do any good whatsoever. Being wealthy is being something before money ever happens. The word "wealth" has ancient origins, so ancient that the origin of the word "wealth" was coined before money as we now know it was invented. The word "wealth" did not describe the possession of a particular commodity or physical substance. It described the ability to live well and freely.

WEALTH IS AN ATTITUDE, NOT A COMMODITY

The word "wealth" described an attitude, a mentality, a personality. Wealth continues at heart to mean "authority, influence, dominion." And when we apply the word "wealth" to ourselves, it means having a high degree of authority, influence, and dominion in our life and in everything that happens to us. It means personal autonomy. It means the ability to support one's self, to express one's self, and to extend one's self independently into the world without having to rely much on anything but the quality of our own consciousness.

People who understand wealth in this way, knowing that this attitude about life can be achieved and that they have a right to achieve it, are wealthy people. The creative power we call God rises up in their consciousness as intelligence in response to this commitment and tells them how to think, how to act, and how to react profitably.

To experience this phenomenon, we don't have to become perfect, we don't have to become geniuses. But we do have to learn how to think, act, and react in better-than-average ways. Creative intelligence will fill our consciousness with all the courage, all the certainty, and all the wisdom that it takes to let us draw into our lives all that is required to give us dominion.

One of these requirements is money. Money was invented to encourage and support whoever or whatever is bringing value to the world. Money gives us something to use so we don't have to stop to cut the grass or paint the house. We can use money to pay somebody else to do those things for us. Then we can be free to do what we do best in bringing value to the world. Money sets us free to be happier, live better, and give more.

But there are other things that wealthy people develop in support of their consciousness. One of these things is a greater-than-average amount of courage and endurance. Wealthy people, people who are going to perform in a better than average way and make more out of life than the typical person, are always those who have the courage to pursue a hot idea and the endurance to stay with it, even when it doesn't seem to be working as fast as everybody else thinks it should.

Wealthy people often have a greater amount of generosity and loyalty toward other people. They know something about themselves that makes it possible to sidestep the fear of theft or abuse in any form. They realize that they know how to get more of every good thing.

Most wealthy people also tend to have a greater-than-average ability to see issues quickly and to make points clearly. Their minds are focused, and not cluttered up with unproductive or counterproductive ideas and fears. They often seem to have a sense of self-confidence that inspires the confidence of other people.

These attributes tend to draw wealthy people into activities that are personally satisfying and financially successful. They also attract the kinds of opportunities, cooperation, and support that it takes to go on to better things. But, given all this, we cannot define wealth in terms of how much money a person holds. There are many people living in very comfortable circumstances who do not have an enormous amount of money. And there are many people with scads of money who are living very poorly and fearfully indeed.

So, wealth really isn't a matter of how much money a person has. Wealth can be defined only in terms of how well and how freely a person lives with whatever amount of money he or she has. Truly wealthy people are those who, by-and-large, are able to do what they want to do, when they want to do it, in a manner that pleases them, with the people with whom they want to do it. These people are wealthy.

There are many, many people who fit into this category. Among them are some with huge amounts of money and others who have little cash on hand at any given time. But whatever the amount of money, they have enough to enjoy their lives in a way that pleases them. And as their concept of what they want to do expands, so will their income or whatever else it takes to help them grow into that richer experience.

Many people with lots of money are not wealthy. They are not wealthy because, for all their money, they are unable to do what they want to do, when they want to do it, the way they want to do it, and with whom. They have paid a high price for their money, the price of being beholden to and limited by people, places, things, events, emotions, and fears. Their concept of wealth is not a spiritual one. It is a materialistic one. They are caught up in coercing the dollar, not in liberating the spirit. Their concept of wealth is built upon figuring how to get money, how to hold onto it, and how to use it to buy more than it's worth. Many of them get so fearful, so hateful, or so sick that no amount of money will set them free to do what they want to do, when they want to do it!

NO MYSTERY IN GETTING MONEY

How to get money is no mystery, if that is all we want to do. We can rob a liquor store. This will get us money but no freedom in its use. And we may lose the freedom we already have. Getting money has nothing to do with wealth. Neither is hanging on to money or trying to use it to get more than it's worth. This is a worrisome pursuit of a narrow-minded objective. It causes people to surrender all their independence and joy, all their time and energy, and all their imagination to getting or making money.

The mind that is fixed on manipulating the outer loses touch with the inner. It is a mind misdirected, a mind that no longer draws upon its own source for power. It no longer draws to itself the power that creates an image of the self as a divinely independent being, able to live without fear, without stress, strain, or limitation. It does not create an image of one's self as divinely created with much to give to the world. There is not a consciousness of wealth, because a conscious of wealth is primarily a consciousness of giving.

A consciousness of wealth is a consciousness that goes forward without fear and without waiting for something to happen to guarantee success. This is the consciousness that gives us the freedom to do what we want to do, when we want to do it, in the style in which we want to do it, and with the people with whom we want to do it. And through this consciousness, the truly rich will always get richer, just as certainly as the dedicated poor will always get poorer.

THE RICH DO GET RICHER AND
THE POOR DO GET POORER

The truly rich will always get richer, and the dedicated poor—because the poor are most certainly dedicated to their poverty—will always get poorer. The poor will always get poorer, no matter how much money is given to them. And the rich will always get richer, no matter how much money is taken away from them. Both poverty and wealth are states of consciousness by which money is either repelled or attracted. This will happen no matter how we try to manipulate circumstances to make things better. The only thing that can change these circumstances is a change of consciousness.

Poverty is a disease, and wealth is the power that will heal it. Someone once said that being broke is a temporary inconvenience, but being poor is a permanent state of mind. There is nothing really wrong with having no money as long as you do not think of yourself as "a poor person"—as long as you do not think of yourself as deprived by life, by society, by family, by neighborhood, by race, by nationality, or by anything else. As long as you do not see yourself as defective, inferior, and created by God to work hard and have little, or as a person who has failed to accomplish, or worse yet, as having done some dreadful thing that means being condemned to learn the lesson of struggling for your daily bread. That's diseased thinking! It is impoverished thinking that no amount of money will heal.

A consciousness of wealth is the only power that will heal it. This consciousness becomes creative in your life when you think about yourself abundantly. This consciousness of wealth works for you creatively when you learn to think about yourself in terms of your intrinsic value and what you can do that is really good and unique to you. In terms of how well you can do it, and in terms of how commited you are to the happy purpose of finding within yourself a better way to relate to the world-at-large. This is a consciousness of wealth! It is powerful! This is the only thing that heals the mental disease of poverty!

When we talk about becoming valuable in the world, we're not talking only about going to your job and doing it better. That's part of it, of course. But there are a lot of wealthy people who don't have jobs. They don't need them. So, we're not merely talking about being a good employer or a good employee. We're talking about how we conduct our thinking about ourselves and the way we speak about ourselves. We're talking about the way we approach everything and everyone we deal with, with an eye toward entering each situation by bringing value to it.

THE GIVERS AND THE TAKERS OF THE WORLD

Some people have estimated that roughly 20 percent of the population of this world approach life as people trying to make something out of it and bring something to it, while 80 percent approach life as poor souls desperately needing to get something out of it, because they believe they have little to give.

Now, the 20 percent are people who do, indeed, make something in the world for themselves. One of the things they make is money. They make it not only for themselves, but they also create opportunities useful to others who are looking in a prospering direction. So, theirs is not a selfish endeavor. These 20 percent who approach life with an attitude of wealth, wanting to make something better out of life, do. The other 80 percent who approach life needing to get something out of it for themselves never do.

And they never will, because the best thing life can ever give us is the power of our own minds, which we already have. In other words, we already have the best thing we are ever going to get. So, life is not about getting anything better. Life is about making better use of the best. Life is about doing better with the best, the best that we already have. These 80 percent are rejecting the best that life has to offer from the start.

The 20 percent are the people who support the world, carrying the burden of what the 80 percent can't bring themselves to bear. It is not that the 80 percent are useless or have no value. It is just that they don't know it. They don't see themselves correctly. Everyone has varying degrees of value, making varying degrees of contributions. But the 80 percent, through ignorance alone, are neither vital nor essential. And the world never rewards them greatly.

Never think that any living soul in this world has no value. We have value at all times, even if it is only as potential. Our value may be only to serve as a horrible example for other people. We always need people for Mother to point at when she says, "Look, Jimmy, do you want to be like *that*?"

In any national economy, the real productivity comes

from 20 percent of the population. In any industry, the real growth is generated by only 20 percent of the people involved in it. In any organization, the essential work, the basic financial support, is provided by 20 percent of the membership. And here is where divine justice shows its golden perfection. Eighty percent of the money in the world is in the hands of that 20 percent of the population. And the other 20 percent of the money is spread very thinly among the 80 percent of the population. The ones who approach life as getters, not givers, do get something, but far less than they could if they understood the power of wealth. The ones who approach life as givers get rich. That is why the rich really do get richer and the poor really do get poorer.

MOVE INTO THE TWENTY PER CENT

Make it your prosperity purpose to become a 20 percenter. Bless yourself and bless the world, too. In the process of moving more and more into that 20 percent you may contribute to enlarging the proportion to 21 percent some day. If we could change that 20 percent to 21 or 25, the entire economy of this world would be profoundly improved. Poverty, starvation, and disease would be enormously relieved. Even the remaining 75 percent would raise up in status, if only just a little. What an impact!

Let's make it our resolve to use the power of wealth to grow wealthy. How do we do that? We do it primarily in spiritual ways, followed by practical ways. We develop a greater, more powerful idea of what wealth truly is and what it is not. We involve ourselves in developing a way of thinking and affirming that instills these ideas into our consciousness. In this way we transform our thoughts by thinking healthier and wealthier.

We also need to monitor the way we talk about money and the way we act with money. We want to be very certain that what we are saying and doing is consistent with the ideas we are embracing in the privacy of our own minds. The soul is witness to the act as well as to the word. Even the best and most persistent and eloquent mental work will be utterly neutralized in the soul by things we say and do in our daily life that contradict it.

PRACTICAL ACTIONS FOR WEALTH

Let me give you some practical ideas that will support your wealth. First of all, it is imperative that you take yourself in hand and insist that you stop looking for free and cheap. When you are looking for free and cheap, you are saying, "I'm not worth very much." And your consciousness accepts this idea about you and creates for you accordingly.

Stay out of the bargain basements and away from fire sales. If you feel you must shop at a discount store, do it, but do not make a religion out of it. Move up to quality stores at the earliest possible moment.

When I say do not make a religion out of it, I mean, do not defend it by saying, "Really! This discount stuff is just as good.'' That statement is perfect nonsense; it is not ''just as good'' at all. Stop looking for ''free,'' and stop looking for ''cheap.'' Shop for quality, and pay the price.

Second, save some portion of all money you receive, even if only a nickel. See this savings as an investment in yourself. Stop being the kind of individual who works and works to earn money, then lets it all go right back out. This is a very poor statement about yourself and your sense of personal worth. Start investing money in yourself. If you can't think of yourself as a good investment, no one else can either.

Don't save for a rainy day. Save for a sunny day. Save so you can stop being someone who constantly misses an opportunity for something wonderful just because you don't have any money available. Stop being the person who says, ''Oh, I can't do that until the income tax check comes in.'' Begin to build money that will be always available. This will do a world of good for your self-esteem and your vision of the future.

Next, pay for everything you use. Pay for it on time, and pay for it cheerfully, even if you have to paste that smile on. If you can't pay for it, or if you resent paying for it, don't use it. Have the dignity not to use it. But if you must use it, then pay for it, and praise it for whatever good it is worth to you.

Pay even for things that you don't get billed for. Don't stiff waiters or cab drivers or whomever. This is actually cheating them. If you are concerned about poor service, call the manager and complain. Otherwise, tip the waiter. You are using that person's time and energy so you need to pay for it.

This goes for church, too. Churches don't bill. Therefore, a lot of people think that they can slink in and slink out without supporting the church. But you cannot create an image of wealth within yourself when you persist in taking something for nothing. If you are getting nothing out of your church, don't go. If you go, pay for what it takes to keep your church going.

Next, find a good cause, a charity, that does something which you think is wonderful and valuable. Then support it with your money. That's how you can enlarge yourself greatly. Find a good cause, something that appeals to your soul, and support it on a regular basis. And do it quietly, please. This is not for show; this is for grow! When we do this sort of thing, we are buying a great and prosperous blessing for ourselves. We are becoming investors in a universe of goodness. It is very important to the self-concept to think of oneself as a person who is investing in something worthwhile for a good and noble cause.

And finally, never, never refuse money or anything of value, including a free lunch, a free ride, a ticket to the ballgame. Never! This is always a sign of wealth trying to find you. This is what you are looking for. Never refuse it. If it is freely and graciously offered, freely and graciously accept it. If you can't use it, pass it on to someone who can. Keep value moving and flowing. And keep yourself open at both ends all the time.

How will you know you are becoming wealthy? You won't know by the amount of income you have or the money in your pocket. Don't bother to sit around counting your pounds and pence like Scrooge. You can't measure your wealth in that way. The amount you have on hand doesn't tell you a single thing as far as wealth is concerned. Money can go much faster than it comes.

So, how will you know that you are becoming wealthy? You will know when it dawns upon you one fine day that your life has changed, and that today you are freer to do what you want to do, when you want to do it, in a manner that pleases you, and with the people that you want to do it with. That's how you will know. By that time, you will have moved into the 20 percent of people who are living well. Then you will be wealthy. Because you will be using the power of your mind as the power of wealth in your life. And that power is infallible. You can count on it.

THE POWER OF LOVE

Now we come to the power of life as the power of love. When you begin to regard your thoughts as power and, specifically, when you realize that your thoughts are the power that can change your desire for good into good experience, you begin to understand that loving thoughts going from you toward others will do you more good than such thoughts from others to you. When you learn to make your desire for love expressed in the world through the action of your thoughts, words, and deeds, you are using love as the power of your life and letting love become the substance of your experience.

Love begins with love of self. If you do not have a good opinion of yourself, it is extremely important to get one. But don't think it comes by doing things that make other people think well of you. Their thoughts have no legitimate creative power in your life. The way to have a good opinion of yourself is to learn how to express love in your own thinking. And if you can't express love in your thinking about "some people" or "certain things," spend very little time thinking about them. Rather, discipline yourself to find whatever is good and true and worthy and beautiful. Then take St. Paul's advice from his famous espistle on love: *Think on these things. A mind so committed in love will easily create a consciousness that thinks well of the self through which it is expressing.*

We each have our own desires—private, understandable only by us, never fully expressible to anyone else. What we want in the way of love is known to us alone. And so the power of our own thoughts, of our own beliefs, must fulfill that desire for us alone. The power to fulfill that desire is entirely in our hands. This means that nobody else can give us the love we desire, because nobody else can possibly know what we desire. Nobody can do that, no matter how hard they try and no matter how deeply or desperately they want to.

Remember this the next time you find yourself building a resentment because someone has not anticipated
your desires or sufficiently appreciated your virtues.

LOVE IS FOR THE GIVING

What all this means is that the power of love is not
something we get. It is something to give. We don't
need to get love. We already have it. We just need to
recognize it. It exists within us as the power behind all
of our desires for good. We have to become adept at
letting the power of love fulfill itself in our life and
in our world through ourselves, our thoughts, our
words, our actions, and our reactions. When we learn
how to give love or make love happen through us, we
are satisfied in love. The power of love within us has
then found a way to get out into the world.

EVERYBODY LOVES A LOVER

They say everybody loves a lover. We've heard it
many times. And it is very true, because every action
generates a reaction that corresponds to it exactly.
That's why everyone must love a lover. And they also
say, *"To him who loves much, much is forgiven."* This is
also true, because love always compels more devotion
than any other human quality. This is why some
people seem to be able to get away with all sorts of outrageous behavior. When a person is perceived as a
love-bringer, a love-giver, people tend to overlook a lot

of other things, a lot of flaws—flaws in appearance, flaws in conduct, even flaws in character.

When your focus is on knowing that you have love and that you intend to give love, you will find fulfillment in love, no matter what. Years ago, during my turbulent youth, when looking for love was my primary occupation, and when my mind was on nothing higher than my latest haircut, I had a friend named Freddy. I liked to go out looking for love with Freddy because Freddy was kind of homely. I always figured that, even on my worst day, I looked pretty good next to him. It took me a while to realize that Freddy was doing much better at love than I ever did. I couldn't understand it. I chalked it up to the bad taste of the world at large. It was absolutely humiliating. Night after night, Freddy had one spectacular conquest after another. And I was left sitting alone. You know how you feel when you see through the barroom window that daylight is coming and you're still there? That was me. And it wasn't until many years later that I understood what was happening. Freddy was a love-giver, and I was a love-seeker. Freddy used the power of love as if he had a lot of it, so he made love happen around him. As you know, anything that happens around you will always include you in it if you let it. Freddy let it. Now, I didn't think I had any love at all. That was my constant whine. So I was languishing about, waiting for people to give me their love in exchange for my wit and beauty and ease. I don't know how much I had of the first two, but I had a lot of the last!

I can remember Freddy getting ready to go out. I

thought he was so silly. He would stand in front of his mirror and pull in his gut, flex his muscles, and look in the mirror and say, ''Oh, boy, someone is going to be glad to see me tonight. Whoever you are, have I got a real treat in store for you.'' It was outrageous! It was so embarrassing to stand there and watch this poor, homely fellow doing this. But, you see, Freddy had learned how to do good, creative mental work years ahead of me. And it worked!

THERE IS MORE TO LOVE THAN ROMANCE

Of course, there is much more to love than romance. And the power of love can bring us much more than a deliriously happy sex life. Everyone knows this. However most of us would prefer to begin with the deliriously happy sex life and catch up to the rest of it later. But it doesn't work that way. The power of love is ultimately regulated by a perfect creative intelligence which seems to know that for life to be secure and for love to be secure, first things must come first.

This means that we must become secure in love in our bread-and-butter relationships. These are the ones that continue day in and day out and carry the weight of our existence. We must be secure in our bread-and-butter relationships before we can be secure in our jam-and-jelly relationships.

Granted, a very nice sex life can be a finishing touch in the life of one who knows how to give love to his neighbor in a neighborly way, to co-workers, employers, and employees in an appropriate way, to family in the right way, and to strangers in need. But effective and satisfactory sexual loving must be the icing on the cake. You have to have a good cake to carry alot of icing. A steady diet of nothing but icing will make you very, very sick and will probably give you pimples, along with who knows what else.

So, with that acknowledged, let us put sex and romance aside for the moment, and let us speak of the power of love as a universal, all-inclusive power. Let us understand that since the greater idea always includes and supports all lesser ideas, we will not be done out of a good sex life or high romance if, for a time, we will lift our minds above our loins, and put them between our ears where they seem to work best anyhow.

Let's consider a great old saying: *Love makes the world go around.* It is a sweet sentiment, and it is also a statement of absolute truth! Love quite literally does make the world, and I mean the planet earth, go around on its axis. Love also makes every other planet in our galaxy go around. Furthermore, love makes all life everywhere move along doing whatever needs to be done to keep life intact. This includes whatever needs to be done to improve life; whatever needs to be done to keep life renewing itself, growing, and expanding. The power of love is always on the move within every living thing, including you and me. Whenever the power of love finds a creative outlet, it passes through and makes something good happen. This happens every single time, whenever and wherever it finds an outlet.

Every cell in your body is constantly purifying itself and reproducing itself, impelled by the power of love: the power of life desiring to live better. Every idea and emotion in your mind and heart is the power of love seeking to drive you to give more to your world and to think of your world, including yourself, in a better way. As this happens, you are moved to do something better for yourself and for whoever else is in your life in whatever relationship.

Learn that love is a power that you already have, and not a commodity that you have to get. Then you will be able to provide an outlet for love on an ongoing basis. And love will come more easily to you as it moves more easily through you.

YOU ARE ALWAYS FULL OF LOVE

Whoever you are, you are always full of love. Love is always pressing itself upon you, wanting you to express it, so it can become something great through you. This is what pious folks mean when they tell us, *"God loves you in spite of yourself."* This is what the great mystic Meister Eckhart meant when he told his detractors, who were telling him God was angry at him because of his heresy, *"I know that God always loves me because that's the way He is. He has no choice in the matter."*

Love isn't a reward we receieve when we become good. Love is the essence of our being, no matter how we're acting. It is the power of goodness that is always in us, ready to let us make something more out of it.

Love is not the result of goodness—it is the cause of goodness. This is the crux of the matter. If things aren't very good with you right now, you can change your experience if you will do some loving. The only way you and I can get goodness in our lives and in our work and in our relationships is to understand how to use the power of love better than we ever have before. We must learn to use the power of love to think properly about our desire for love and how to approach life as givers, not merely takers.

Many otherwise intelligent people are confused when it comes to love. They know they are supposed to give love. They've been told that since they were knee high to a grasshopper. But they are waiting until they get a huge pile of it stored away before they are willing to spare a little of it. And they certainly don't intend to give love to anyone who doesn't deserve it. And most often, their standards for people who deserve it are much higher than their standards for themselves. It never occurs to them that the undeserving need love much more than the deserving do. Furthermore, they are not going to give love to anyone who might not give it back to them. They think it's a losing proposition.

THE URGE IS TO GIVE IT

These people are not stupid, but they do not understand what I call "the urgency of love." They incorrectly think that the urge for love is an urge to get it. Therefore, they completely misinterpret the love urge.

Love is not an emptiness longing to be filled—it is a fullness pressing to be released. It is the power, the creative energy of love, bristling with activity and very much in need of an outlet, a place to flow to and something to become.

This energy is like the power of electricity. If it flows out, it can light up the world. If it has no outlet, it will eventually burn its circuits and throw us into darkness and despair. And that's exactly what happens to all too many of us for all too long.

The giving of love, the universal giving of love, the unconditional giving of love, is not a nicety. It is a necessity. It is not something sweet you can plan to do someday when your life is great and you have everything plus time to spare. It is something that absolutely must be done by every one of us if we are ever going to come to the point where our lives are really worth living.

We need to move our thinking away from the ''get'' verb and over to the ''give'' verb when we think about love. When we know we have to give it, we will find a way. And it won't be hard. But when we think we must get it, we have no control over it at all. We act like poor creatures wandering around, waiting for something to drop into our souls. This usually leads us to do some foolish, frustrating, and desperate things, to become very weary from the chase or dreary from the wait.

If you want to see how misdirected people are about love, just watch the way they act, and listen to what they say and sing about love. How many people talk about love constantly when they are happily engaged in loving? How many happy songs do you know about love versus how many sad songs? How many people do you think approach romance like my friend Freddy?

GO OUT EACH DAY AND GIVE IT!

How many people do you know who get up each morning and decide what they are going to give their life to that day? How many people get up, brush their teeth, comb their hair, and say, "What can I bring to my world today?" How many people board a bus, enter a restaurant, or come into the midst of a new social situation thinking about what they can do for the people they're going to meet there? I'm not talking about giving them money. I'm just talking about things like a quick smile or a loving glance. Most people enter situations like that wondering what people will think of them and thinking of little else.

How many people do you think give regular thought to finding a way to forgive an old debt, or to let up on an ancient grudge or resentment, by doing or saying something loving to or about the debtor or the grudgee? How many people do that just for the sake of doing it? Just to clear the air and get that burden off their minds? How many people do you think will go to work tomorrow and refuse to pick up yesterday's argument but will inject something new and better into that situation instead? You know, no argument can continue if one of the persons stops arguing. And only when that happens, does love have a chance.

Performing such deeds constitutes the giving of love. Anyone can start loving in these ways at any time. It doesn't cost a dime. Nothing has to happen first, and you don't need anyone's permission.

STOP FAILING AT LOVE

We don't fail to give love because we are mean and hateful. We are not mean and hateful. We are essentially good people. We fail to give love because we are afraid or shy or feel awkward. And mostly because we are thoughtless. We tend to be thoughtless because we are not conditioned to believe that our thoughts are important. We have never really thought of our love as power, the power that can transform our desire into our experience.

There are many reasons why we do not use the power of love well. However, none of them are *good* reasons. No matter what the excuse, our failure to do so denies us the expression of the eternal urging of our soul—to grow by the ongoing giving of love.

It is always right to love! It is always right to express the power of love. Loving will never hurt you. Love expressed will bypass all those people who can't accept it and find its way directly to all those who can. It will bring into your life a much better cast of characters than you could ever imagine. So, there's never anything to be lost. Your expression of love might be lost on some, but it will never be lost on you.

It is always right to love. Don't let anyone tell you

differently, including those people who think they "love too much." They are not in trouble because they love too much. They are in trouble because they manipulate too much and love too little. They are in trouble because they are emotionally confused. Now, this is not a gender problem. It is neither a female problem nor a male problem. It's a consciousness problem. And it's not about loving too much. It's about knowing too little about the power of love and how it works.

Love makes the world go round. It is the power of life desiring to be lived beautifully. It wants to make your life more beautiful and more joyful by becoming the power of your mind as you think about your heart's desires. So learn to let the power move through you and give it all you've got.

THE POWER OF WORK

Work is the fourth corner of the foundation of a well-balanced life. We need to view our work as our power. This concept can be puzzling at first because we generally do not think of work as giving us power. We generally think of it as something that dissipates power or depletes the worker. That is why so many people drag themselves home from work, exhausted instead of exhilarated, irritated instead of satisfied. They tend to isolate themselves from the world instead of being eager to get out there and enjoy some of their well-earned money and well-earned leisure time. Isn't it pathetic that we don't take advantage of what we work for?

Years ago in New York City, one of the daily tabloids ran a photo across a double-page spread. The shot was taken of a row of people from the shoulders up, full face toward the camera. Nothing indicated where they were or what they were doing. This picture was published as part of a contest in which the public was invited to guess who the people were and why they were all together. The people were of all ages, genders, and races. It was quite a mix. But every single one of them looked anything from grim and angry to absolutely terror-stricken. They were the most frightening looking bunch of people you ever saw in your life.

Thousands of people responded to the contest, but not one got the right answer. The most common guess was that these were displaced persons in a refugee camp lined up for their shots and papers before relocation. Others guessed that these people were mental patients lined up to be taken on an outing. The tabloid published the full-length picture on the day the results were announced. Neither refugees nor mental patients, these people were New York City commuters photographed during rush hour. They were lined up at the curb outside Grand Central Station waiting for the light to change so that they could cross the street and go to work.

Not one of these people was wearing a look of joyful anticipation. Not one looked as if he or she were going forward to express power. Because, of course, they weren't. They were going forward to be worn down, stressed out, and used up by their jobs. They knew it, and they looked it! Like so many others, they did not think of work as empowering but as depleting. As a result, they worked under too much pressure and not nearly up to their potential.

The pressure in our work is never in the job. It is always within the consciousness of the worker. We must get clear on that. We need to understand that the job doesn't exist until we walk in, turn on the lights, and sit at the desk or the machine, or wherever we are working. That job does not exist without us. It is simply waiting there. And everything that job is, is brought to it by the person who performs it. The worker brings the stress, the worry, all of the negative baggage, and whatever skill, value, or excellence that goes into it or comes out of it.

YOU ARE NOT YOUR JOB

If you ask most people who they are, they will tell you what they do. Try it whenever you meet new people. They'll say, ''I'm the librarian down at the branch library,'' or ''I'm the manicurist at the hair salon,'' or ''I'm the attorney up the street.'' We tend to think that our work defines us, that it justifies us, that it explains us, that it makes something out of us that is more than we really are.

This is not correct at all.

You are always infinitely greater than even the greatest job or even the most prestigious career. Because you are the power that makes it happen. No job really brings dignity or status to anyone. If we have any dignity or any status, we don't get it from our work. We bring it to our work. We express it through the process of doing our work, any kind of work. Dignity comes from how we do our work, not from the kind of work we do. As a matter of fact, until we can work with dignity, expressing the excellence of our being in whatever work we are doing now, we will never convince ourselves, or anyone else, that we will be able to do well in a more prestigious career.

This is a good point to make with anyone who is goofing off or whining about how good he or she would be if someone would only provide a better opportunity. I always want to ask questions like these of such people: *"If you can be that good, why aren't you being that good right now? You're taking your employer's money, aren't you? You're going there every day, aren't you? If you're that good, why don't you show it where you are now?"*

Many people are walking around thinking that they are better than their jobs. The truth is, they probably are. But because they don't want to show it, we can never really know for certain. Only when they show it through the way they perform is anyone else going to realize it and then reward it. And only then will they themselves believe it enough to move up to a better opportunity.

GET OUT OF IT BY GETTING INTO IT

The only creative way to get out of a dull, limiting job is to grow out of it. You can get out of it in many other ways. You can walk off in a pout and quit. You can always get yourself fired. But that's not creative because people who do that always wind up in another dull, boring job. Although those methods may be convenient, they create nothing. The only creative way to grow out of it is to get into it. Then, when you truly become too good for your job, consciousness will create another one for you and move you to it.

Real dignity and status originate in the consciousness of the individual and blossom in a job or a career as power succeeding. And whoever has real dignity and status will look good and feel happy and fulfilled in whatever he or she is doing. Dignity does not come from simply having a job that society says is better or more important or more glamorous than another. The file clerk who is competent and reliable has more real dignity and status than the brain surgeon who is careless, or the stockbroker who is crooked, or the minister who cannot practice what he preaches.

WHAT WE THINK OF OURSELVES
ALL DAY LONG IS WHAT COUNTS

As mentioned above, most people, when asked who they are, will tell you what they do. And since so many of them don't like what they do and don't get much

joy out of it, they don't think much of themselves
either. Nor do they enjoy their lives as much as they
should. This is both sad and dangerous to their personal well-being, since what we think of ourselves all
day long is our creative design. What we think of ourselves all day long, not just now and then, is the design that our consciousness follows in plotting the
events and circumstances of our lives. It designs what
we are going to do and what is going to happen to us.

Many people work extremely hard to make good
things happen, and then get nothing out of all that
good work. That's pathetic! There are people who
work long and hard to rise in their work but who are
not able to draw power from their lofty positions. They
never feel really competent, really secure, or at ease.
They do not live better because of what they do. They
use up all of their power attaining those positions, trying to hold on to the job, and trying to get the work
done. In truth, they believe that the job is too big for
them; they see the job as more important than they
are. And there they sit in carpeted corner offices, not
feeling any better about themselves than do many
other people, far from corner offices or carpets or any
other symbols of prestige or power. And they say, "I
felt better when I was down working on the line."
Well, they didn't! They were the biggest whiners and
complainers in the world when they were down on the
line. They've just forgotten. They were unfulfilled
then, and they are unfulfilled now. Because the thing
they thought would fulfill them has not done so. They

changed tactics, but they did not change their consciousness of work.

UNDERSTAND THE TRUTH
ABOUT THE POWER OF WORK

If struggling to get a good job or to build a prestigious career does not make our work a power for good in our lives, then what does?

We must understand the truth about power, all power. Power is always something you bring to a situation in order to make something greater out of it. The power we bring to our work is the idea that this work is our opportunity to serve, rather than our opportunity to get something we are lacking. This work is our opportunity to do something worthwhile in a way that is uniquely particular to us. We must see our work as our opportunity to give and to create something good. It must not be seen as what we have to do to make a living so we can keep going and get somewhere in the world. We must approach work as a person of power, not in the hopes of becoming such a person.

You and I and all people everywhere have a tremendous need—a God-implanted need to be of service to each other. We have it even when we get mad at each other. We have it even when we pout and say, "I'm not going to do anything for anybody." This need never goes away because it is essential to our nature. It is part and parcel of our nature to be of service to each other. We have a need to do whatever we can to make it possible for all of us to live more comfortably, more securely, more healthfully, and more joyfully. Unless we believe that in some way we are doing that, we really don't think much of ourselves.

We have this need simply because we are alive. In our true heart we love life, and we will never feel as secure and happy about life as we want to unless we are serving the living in some way, doing something that pleases us and makes us proud of ourselves.

ALL WORK IS SERVICE TO OTHERS

So, all work is service to others. *All* work! All work serves some good purpose. Otherwise, that job would not exist, and nobody would pay a cent for it. You say, "Well, it's not a high enough purpose for me." Well, then, why can't you do it right? If it's too simple for you, why can't you do it right? You must be able to do the simple work right before you can do the complicated.

All work is valuable service. Whatever work you find before you is your opportunity to fulfill your God-implanted need to be of service. That's what it is all about, whether you know it or not. Any task that you find in front of you at any moment is your opportunity to grow in power by being true to your own creative urge to serve in this world.

When we know this about work, all work, whatever we do well becomes a power for good in our lives. Through our work, we become more productive, more valuable to the world, and more secure within ourselves. Then, we know that not only are we doing something that fulfills our needs and fills somebody else's need as well, but that we are in control of our own destiny. We are not just wishing and hoping to be recognized and regarded. We are guaranteeing it.

YOU ARE ALWAYS SELF-EMPLOYED

No matter what kind of work you do, no matter what company name is over the door that you walk through on Monday morning, no matter who signs the check that you pick up on Friday afternoon, you are always self-employed. The best workers in any field at any level either know this or sense it—and they act like it.

The person who must be satisfied with the quality of your work is *you*. Your work will be a great power for good in your life when you are, for the most part, satisfied with everything you are doing. When you are not satisfied, no matter what the reason, there is something missing for you. And that is a sense of dignity, a sense of security, a sense of challenge. What is missing is the true reward you should be getting from what you are doing.

You are always self-employed because you are working primarily to fulfill your own God-implanted need to be of service to the world. And when this need becomes the focus in our work, all other things will come along as a matter of course. All the money! All the promotions! All the perks! All the prestige! All these things will naturally follow. You are really not working for any of these things, they are all the world's way of working for you when it senses that you are working for it. All of these things come to us when we are working to express our creative ability through our work.

FALSE WORK ATTITUDES

Certain widespread work attitudes are false and self-defeating. Perhaps the strongest of these is the belief that work must be hard in order to be valuable, that we must work hard in order to be successful. By "hard," I mean stressful, tiring, frustrating, dragging-home, beat-to-a-pulp-every-night kind of work. But stress, exhaustion, and frustration are all negative ideas and negative conditions, and they have no value within themselves. Being valueless, they cannot lead to productive performance at work.

Instead of looking for ways to work hard, we need to look for ways to work easily and joyfully, intelligently and creatively. Ease and joy and intelligence have great value within themselves. And when we can bring them into the workplace, we will always increase our productivity. Coming home at night cross, exhausted, and muddle-headed, does not indicate that a good day's work was done. More than likely it indicates that you were not nearly as productive as you could have been.

Many people want more pay because they work under stress and strain and because their jobs make them worry a lot. "They don't understand; my job's hard; it's very stressful; I want a raise." Well, I don't think these people should get more pay for being stressed out. I think they should probably get less, because stress and strain and worry aren't in the job description. It's not part of the job. It is in the consciousness of these people, in their attitudes about work, and when they bring these attitudes to their work, I believe it cuts productivity. I believe that the only thing we should get paid for is for what we produce, not how sick and tired it makes us.

Several years ago, the air traffic controllers called an illegal strike for more money. They said that their job was stressful and made them very nervous and agitated. They didn't propose how getting more money would make them less nervous and agitated. They wanted more pay for being less effective than they should have been in the job. That's what it came down to. Now, I am not at all certain we should pay money to keep nervous, agitated people in control towers at airports. It's like going to a brain surgeon and saying, "How much for this operation?"

And he says, "Well, most brain surgeons would charge ten thousand, but I charge twenty thousand."

"Well, why?" you might ask.

"Because that operation makes me so nervous."

WE NEED TO BE OUR BEST AT ALL TIMES

In our work, our part is not to succeed. Our part is to keep trying and to do our best. Life's job, God's job, is to succeed. Life will succeed anywhere a good effort is being made. If we understand this, we are set free to do the best that we can do. As we do what we really can, God does what the Creator must: God makes us successful. We are always working at becoming the people life succeeds through in its eternal purpose. And what is life's eternal purpose? It is to serve the living in better and better ways and to make life more of a happy experience for people all the time. When we view any work we do in this manner, that work becomes a power for good in our lives and helps us prosper in all ways.

PART THREE
POWER—THE PRACTICE

The concept of mental or spiritual healing has been around for a long time. People are intrigued by the idea that they have the power within themselves to achieve what nobody else, including the experts, can do. In spite of this interest, and in spite of the fact that many people have achieved what they have aspired to by means of mental or spiritual healing, the practice has never been totally respectable. It is not necessarily an interest that you'd admit to some of your friends. Even though many people would really like to believe that spiritual healing can work, and really do hope that somebody will make it respectable enough for them to believe in and practice openly, they find it hard to become personally committed to it for long.

They are, instead, waiting for someone to make it more palatable to them or to give them assurances that it always works so that they can apply it with confidence. In truth, mental/spiritual healing always does work, but only for those who learn how to work with it and then practice it.

The concept of mental or spiritual healing has never

enjoyed universal acceptance because it requires much more from people than most believe they can give. That is, it requires people to use their own minds and to respect their own intelligence more than they believe they really ought to and, therefore, more than they can ever give themselves permission to do. It requires people to rise up to their personal power in a world that has steadfastly conditioned them to think of real power as something we humans don't have at hand, but as something that must come from somewhere "out there." Thus, the world loads people with responsibility but deprives them of a sense of power. That's quite unfair when you stop to think about it. If you went to work and your employer said, "You're responsible for getting this work done and for doing it perfectly," but gave you no materials to work with, no back-up, and no instruction, you would have little chance of succeeding. You could only plug along and hope for the best. Well, that is exactly how most people deal with the issues in their lives. They plug along and hope for the best.

Culture, religion, and the best of political, theological, social, and economic theory condition us to look to the "great beyond" for all the good we need or are likely to get. We are encouraged to look to "them," to listen to what "they say," or to hope "they" will do something to help us. It's in our language. Listen closely and you will hear yourself speaking this way. You will certainly hear other people talk about being disappointed in life because of "them," by what "they" are doing, by what "they" are not doing, and

by what "nobody" seems to understand. We are conditioned to look to the the great beyond for our good
by putting in our requisition for it, hoping that there's
enough to go around, and hoping that we are worthy
of it. And, at that, we think we must have the help of
others doing more for us than we think we can do for
ourselves.

We are led to believe that the great beyond, that
realm of power and goodness and abundance that is
out there somewhere, is presided over by some deity
who is the ultimate authority deciding who gets what
and what happens to whom. This deity has power of
pardon, power of amnesty, and certainly power of
veto, but it is not involved in the day-to-day activity of
getting good things done. In other words, the great
deity may mess something up for cause but is not
really involved in guaranteeing much good. This
supreme creative authority is so far removed and so
unpredictable that it is best not to disturb "him," except in extreme situations when we've reached the end
of our rope, all else has failed, and there is nothing else
to lose.

In our daily lives, however, we believe that the
power we seek for our healing and blessing and
prospering has been divinely delegated to God's
subalterns here on earth.

God's subalterns on earth are not necessarily the
clergy. Many people have stopped going to them to
seek wisdom, because a lot of people don't expect too
much of them. Therefore, many of those in the clergy
play a cautioning role rather than a creative one. If

you're a clergyperson or if you have a friend or relative who is, he or she may be a wonderful help to many people. So, don't get insulted by this. There are exceptions to every rule. I'm talking in very general terms about the consciousness of the human race, including our clergy in this particular day and age.

Some people still believe that the clergy have influence over what happens to us in the hereafter, but that they seem to have no influence over our lot in life in the present unless they can get elected to public office. That is why people are staying away from church in droves. Although at one time the clergy were the great teachers of goodness in the school of life, today many are currently no more than hall monitors. Some are able to keep us in line, but they don't necessarily do much for us as far as learning anything new or progressing in our spiritual understanding.

Today, the earthly keepers of the powers of health are primarily the physicians. Through their techniques, their medicines, the impressive equipment they use, they are considered the true conduits of God's medical wisdom. They are supported and supplemented by other superbly trained, well-motivated people in many different service disciplines. And thank God for all of them. We would be in a terrible mess without them. These people deserve our respect because they believe in the healing of one body. They believe in it enough to make a profession out of such healing and to commit their lives to it. They approach health in a particular way, via a particular discipline, and do a great deal of good which otherwise would not be done.

But what most people don't understand and what even most physicians don't fully understand, is that no matter what their practice—whether medicine, surgery, psychiatry, or any other specialty, they are primarily practicing mental or spiritual healing. Their commitment to their work is inspired by the spirit of life within them, operating through them, using the power of their minds to lead them to right understanding and practice.

It is the creative intelligence within them that gives them the wisdom to know what they need to know and the courage to do what they need to do through the healing disciplines they have chosen. No matter what their title or what their practice it is always the wisdom within them that does the work. In other words, it is the intelligence within them that is responsible for whatever healing results from their ministrations. But what they and most other people fail to acknowledge is that all people have access to that same fundamental intelligence. And its universal wisdom will come to every one of us if we are able to understand and accept it.

Mental or spiritual healing is not some sort of weird, other-worldly, naive nonsense. Real mental or spiritual healing is any process by which we learn how to heed the urging of the spirit, the desire to live in wholeness, and to use the power of our intelligence to engage in ideas that have a healing impact on our lives. These ideas may lead us to a good doctor, or away from the wrong doctor, or beyond the current limitations of medicine.

How we go about the business of healing—what our technique or method is—is of very little importance. What matters is that it achieves the desired results. If somebody who has been diagnosed as having an incurable disease goes to a witch doctor and gets cured, nobody is going to say, "Im sorry. That is not the approved method; go get that cancer again and go through the right channels." The "right channel" is the one that heals you. The fact that it heals is evidence that it is the "right" channel. The method is of little importance as long as it produces a healing result without damaging the individual in the process.

THE HEALING POWER REALLY IS WITHIN

Healing occurs because the power that heals everything really is within everyone. The power that lives and keeps on making life worth living lives within all the living, moves through all the living, and provides all the living with ongoing vitality. This power succeeds individually as each person believes it can, expects it to, and allows it to. Thought is the healing activity, and the initial action of this healing power in your life or mine is always our thought about it, our feelings about it, our consciousness of it.

So, if we want to do healing work by mental or spiritual means, the first thing we must heal is the quality of our thought. If we are looking for clarity in our lives, the first thing we must get clear is our consciousness. If we are looking for purity, the first thing to get purified is our mind. If we are looking for vitality in our lives, the first thing we must revitalize is our thinking.

Physicians who turn to the power within, the power of their own thoughts, turn necessarily to the conditioning of their own training. Their help will come, most likely, through a new idea about medical practice, through an insight that leads them to a new way to practice medicine. They find help through medical means because healing power takes shape according to the mentality that seeks it.

The psychiatrist, the chiropractor, the hypnotherapist, the nutritionist—whatever—will get their help, most likely, through an idea related to their specialty, which will improve their practice and lead them to go beyond what they previously thought possible. But if the good they seek does not come in that way, they must not assume there is no healing possible. They must assume that it will come another way, and they must be receptive enough to allow for it. That is the true scientific spirit.

If people with health problems seek help from any person in a physical healing discipline, they need to be certain that the person they rely upon believes that there is a way to heal people and pursues real healing with genuine interest and optimism, whether it originates from their particular discipline or not.

HEAL THE PATIENT, NOT THE DISEASE

Your doctor's emphasis must be on healing you, not killing the disease. You don't heal a person by killing a disease. You heal a person by healing a person. Be very careful that the person helping you is open to new and innovative ideas. This person must believe that the power of life in you is greater than the power of the disease affecting you. This person must be adventurous enough in spirit to rule out nothing in his or her efforts to help you unless he or she suspects that it would be harmful.

This medical/healing professional's primary interest ought to be the healing of your person, and unless they are not going to rule out anything that supports this idea, your chances are limited to what the person knows at present or his or her likes or dislikes. Unfortunately that may not be enough to heal you. If this person's scope is not broad enough, the ability to heal you, save your life, or make it worth living might be too limited. It is criminal to condemn ourselves to death or illness because of what our doctor doesn't know, or what our treating person is not willing to do or think about. But most people do exactly that.

Most people simply do not know that the power that heals is always available and always works for the good of all people through the action of their own thoughts. There are many people in many marvelous healing professions who have developed special ways of using this power that heals. However, this same power is ours. It is available to everyone. The power doesn't know whether or not you went to medical school. The power doesn't know if you specialized in dentistry. It just works through everyone in the way we are able to direct it. So, anyone who makes it his or her business to draw upon a greater wisdom, a greater courage, a greater understanding, and to build a consciousness of healing, can use this power constructively, with or without adequate medical help.

YOU CAN DO IT YOURSELF

If somebody else knows how to do something for you that needs to be done, let that person do it. But if nobody else knows how, you'd better discover a way to do it yourself. You don't have to continue suffering with a disease, and you don't have to die of a disease because of what your doctor or specialist doesn't know. When none of these professional people can help you, God still can, and will, and has every inclination to do so. Why? Because God is the spirit of life. God is the spirit of wholeness that wants to live through you. But you must put more faith in this idea of God, and make as many demands upon such a God as you do your physician.

IT ONLY TAKES THE FAITH YOU HAVE

The amount of faith it takes to work with this creative power within is the amount you already possess. You don't have to reach for more. It's simply a matter of withdrawing your demands and expectations from whoever or whatever says "no" to your well-being and giving them to God.

Many people say, "Oh, I just don't have enough faith." But we all have lots of faith. The question is, "What's it in?" A lot of people have faith that they will get sick at 40 and be dead by 50. They really believe it. Now, that's faith, a lot of faith. It is enough faith to compel exactly that chain of events to happen.

Stop thinking of faith quantitatively. There's not a big bowl of faith that we have to find and take a large portion of. We are all full of faith. Faith is expectancy, and we are always expecting something. The question is, what?

When we talk about developing faith, we do not mean going out and getting it. We mean learning how to direct it and take charge of it. We must think about developing the courage to say to something we've believed in but has always failed us, "I don't believe in you anymore." Then we turn to something that says, "If you work this way, you can have success." And we say, "All right. I choose to believe in you. I choose to believe in you just enough to start to work in that direction." That's how faith in the better gets started. It gets started by having just enough fearlessness to admit that what isn't, isn't, and to believe that there must be something that is.

THE WORLD EXPLAINS MISERY AS MYSTERY

The world's resistance to mental or spiritual healing, or healing through the use of the individual's consciousness, is not based upon experience. Spiritual

healing has not been well-tested and proved unsuccessful. It has never been widely practiced or encouraged. Its success is usually explained away or
ignored.

People who have had a great healing as a result of
consciousness are generally written off as fools or
frauds. Often their healing is discounted as "luck," or
their disease as something that never existed in the
first place or as a misdiagnosis. Their healing is sometimes called a miracle, a mystery, something supernatural.

We tend to relegate what we do not readily understand to the supernatural because, if such is the case,
it's beyond us. Therefore, there is no necessity to try
to understand it. We easily turn to the supernatural
when something conflicts with our traditional opinions
and past experience. Our churches encourage it and
resort to this explanation every time one of their doc-
trines is shown to make no good sense. They say, "It
is so because it is the inspired word of God, so you
must accept it on faith, because you are not equipped
to know better." Without hesitation, we accept routine
misery as mystery, but demand evidence for great new
ideas.

When people are told that there is a simple though
dynamic mental technique that can be used in healing,
they often say something to the effect of, "I don't see
how that will work. Therefore, I don't believe it will
work. My problem isn't that simple. My disease is very
powerful. My difficulty is far too complicated and

rooted deeply within me. So your simple method will never work." And I always want to say, "How do you know if you've never tried?"

Their rejection is not based upon experience. It is based upon a determination to hang on to a belief system that places all power out *there* and all difficulty and suffering *within*. Their fundamental belief is that the world and everything in it is greater than we are, and is more than we can survive when all seems to be against us. So, if someone else better than we are, some expert, can't fix it, it can't be fixed.

But there are and always have been people given up for dead from cancer, for example, who have found within themselves a way to heal themselves and to live on in health for many years. The general public hears little or nothing of this sort of thing because it really doesn't want to. It is never headline news. Most people don't want to hear much about it because it is a challenge to change their thinking.

There are many people today who are living healthfully with the AIDS virus, and some who are outliving the virus. But little is heard about them, and less is really believed. People would rather die than seriously challenge or change their belief systems. Most people are content to wait for a medical solution and are determined that they won't get well without one. They don't want to have to resort to their own power. It would destroy their lives as they have always lived them. But their lives as they have always been lived are exactly what has attracted the disease.

One of the most shocking discoveries to make when

working with seriously ill people is how few of them really want to get better. I am not saying that they don't want to *be* better. I am saying they don't want to *get* better. They would all like to be better as long as they don't have to do very much about it, on the inside. They will go to all sorts of trouble on the outside but will give up nothing of their inner being: their passions, expectations, opinions.

Spiritual or mental healing is for people who have decided that they would rather live and live well even if it means changing their minds. It is for people who are willing to open their minds and their hearts to a lot of things and to give up a lot of nonsense that they should have dismissed years ago. It takes much more courage to undergo this type of healing than to endure pain or poverty or rejection. It takes much more courage to live than to die.

WE HEAL OUR LIVES BY FIRST HEALING OUR MINDS

The Scriptures tell us, *"As a man thinketh in his heart, so is he."* It does not say, *"What* a man thinketh in his heart."* It says *as.* What's being talked about are attitudes or habits of thought—the kinds of ideas that spring up and the kinds of emotions that arise to support those ideas when we hear or see things, or when things happen to us. This is how we "thinketh" in our hearts. And this is what makes our lives take the turns they take regardless of how we struggle to get them to go this way or that. Our lives go the way of our minds.

In real spiritual healing, what must be healed is the overall quality of our habitual thoughts about everything—from God, the creative power of all life, to ourselves and what we as individuals are doing with that power through the agency of our deep, true, and individual thought. We don't heal our lives by praying to get rid of particular problems or conditions. We heal our lives by creating a consciousness that believes that God is the only real power in the universe and the only real power in our lives, and that this power supports our desire for healing and operates in our lives on every level to let that be so.

We must understand from the beginning that, if there is anything wrong in our body, in our relationships, in any aspect of our physical world, it is always the exact reflection of something that has been very wrong for some time in our heart, in our consciousness, in our real, deeply held attitudes about what and who we are. It reflects our attitudes about what life and God and the world are all about and what we have a right to expect. Our problems are not tied just to a particularly painful incident that happened 32 or however many years ago. They are products of the overall quality of our consciousness.

Many people have an extremely limited view of themselves and what they have a right to expect. Our worst and most destructive attitudes and ideas are too insane to stand up in public and be exposed to the light of day. We learn how to hide them, even from ourselves. We often carry in our hearts those things that would be impossible to justify in our minds. So, since we can't justify them, we bury them. We take them to heart and that is where they work against us. They always impact on the overall quality of our consciousness. They silently subvert the good that comes our way until we learn how to purposefully and habitually generate so much good that it becomes the overpowering tendency in our consciousness.

WE MUST LEARN TO AFFIRM GREAT VALUE

We heal ourselves mentally when we accept and affirm for ourselves great, beautiful, life-loving, life-giving ideas about ourselves. A lot of people run around saying, ''I love music, I love drama, I love ballet.'' I think that's good and certainly better than not liking anything. But, although involvement with such beauty may keep us away from many destructive activities, it will not heal us.

Our healing requires our involvement with a greater love: a love of life-giving ideas about ourselves. We need to persist in finding ways to affirm ourselves, say good things about ourselves, and claim good things for ourselves. We must learn to see the great possibility in our lives not the old experiences. We must keep doing this until the image touches our hearts. At first it won't; at first we'll think we are big frauds. But we must keep it up until it does touch our hearts, until such ideas filter down through our consciousness, through all the nonsense, and take their rightful place in our hearts.

Such a self-image will push out of our belief systems

all that is unlike itself. Because two opposing ideas can't exist at the same time in the same place. The desirable image will always push out the unwanted expectation. Then we will no longer be thinking one way and feeling another.

In this way, our desires become consistent with our expectations. What we want to be true becomes one with what we think ought to be true. No one else can make this happen to us. No one else can choose the kinds of ideas that appeal to us and persistently impose such ideas upon us. We can't go anywhere to get it done for us. Not at any price.

This is the way we bring wholeness or oneness to our consciousness, so that our minds are no longer in conflict with our souls. Our mind is thus healed. What is going into it is what we want to have coming out of it. That's what healing is all about. It is about life at peace with itself. It is about mind believing the best about life. When the power of our mind is thinking in harmony with itself on all levels, a new condition, a new outward expression of our being, is created. We are thus impelled to know what to do, how to act and react, and how to attract all that it takes to build a life that is compelled by such a consciousness.

It is that simple, but not too simple to work. Don't say it's too simple until you've tried it and failed. Although quite simple, it is extremely difficult. We have trouble with simplicity because we mistake pain for complexity and simple solutions for stupidity. The more it hurts, the harder we believe it is to get rid of. But what makes it hurt so much is not what it is, but what we are afraid we are not. Pain comes to alert us to evil. Fear makes a home for it and lets it grow.

IT'S NOT ALL IN YOUR MIND

Mental action must be the primary action in the healing process. This doesn't mean that it's the only action. It means that it's what must come first and lead to all other actions. Mental action must lie behind and underneath, supporting and giving power to everything else we do. Because only mind creates. Only mind can make something out of nothing. Only mental action brings to light the new, the better, the something else that we desire, believe in, and long to see.

There is a difference between the words "*create*" and "*manufacture.*" "Create" means make out of nothing; "manufacture" means make by hand out of something else. Creation, or creating, is entirely a mental activity. It takes place in mind alone. It consists of nothing but thought or mental images. The only things that you and I ever create are thoughts. We don't create money. We don't create automobiles. We don't create houses or jobs or love affairs. We don't create healthy livers or hearts or colons or joints. We don't create pure blood, and we don't create powerful immune systems.

You and I create only the great heartwarming, interest-grabbing, spiritually compelling, life-giving, images or ideas about ourselves. Strong ideas. Pure ideas. Lovely ideas. Since we can do this with nothing but our minds, we can begin the creative process anytime, anywhere, and under any conditions. We don't need anybody else or anything to happen first. We don't need another piece of information or another opinion. All we need is our mind thinking in the right direction. That's creativity. It all begins with mental action. It is always a matter of first knowing something, of getting a good strong image of something, a thorough belief in something, and growing into a love or appreciation of that something.

THE IDEA MUST COME FIRST

Everything that has ever appeared in the physical world was first created as an idea. Nothing will ever come into the physical world, including that which is in our bodies, until we have accepted an idea of it. Whether we have accepted that idea because we have worked with spiritual mind treatment or whether we have accepted it because we were raised to think that way and there's never been much doubt about it in our minds, it makes no difference.

For example, an architect who wants to put up a building must first create an idea of it by deciding on the kind of building and if it is a worthwhile endeavor. The idea has to come first and be accepted. Then the architect objectifies the idea by thinking about it, by developing a plan and coming up with a set of directions that will make the idea understandable to others. It must be very clear to the architect before it can be presented clearly to everyone else.

If the architect is to create the desired structure, then the participation of persons who do not grasp a similar vision, who aren't interested in architecture, who think there are too many buildings already, or who don't approve of the particular design, or who just don't like the architect as a person, cannot be tolerated. These people must not be involved because they will always muddy up the idea. The idea must also be supported by another idea, one that supports and encourages and draws faith from all those who are around. Having created the idea of the building, the architect must keep it fresh by remaining enthusiastic about it and by projecting enthusiasm to all those around. In turn, they will provide encouragement and support.

In this same way, the composer creates a symphony, and the programmer sits down and creates a computer program, and so on. No matter what our objective, the creative process always moves from idea to action, from inner image to outer activity and ultimate manifestation.

This is the way it works throughout all creation. It is even the way it works for the lonely person who wants to make a good friend. To create a good friendship we must first create an image of what a good friend is. We have to sit down, get out of fantasy land, and establish some clear standards for what is acceptable to us in friendship and what definitely is not. What's right is what we want. What's wrong is what we don't. It's our own choice to make and then to live with.

It also works this way for poor people who want to create personal affluence in their lives. They must first get an idea of what personal affluence means to them.

They must see it as something good and good for them. A lot of people don't have money because they've been cursing it all their lives. We curse money when we resent others for having it. Our minds compute resentment as rejection of money, so we cannot get rich while cursing or resenting the affluent. We need to develop an interest in them. They obviously know something of value that we can find out, so it's best to admire what they must know, never mind what they are or are not. That is God's business.

This is also the way it works for the cancer patient who wants a new stomach, one without a tumor attached to it. And this is also the way it works for the AIDS patient who wants a strong immune system.

In every instance, the first step is to create an idea of what is wanted. Create an idea of the thing, because until such an idea is established in your heart, there will never be such a thing in your life. We do not heal ourselves by getting focused upon what we *don't* want, but upon what we *do* want. This is the great difficulty. Anybody can get caught up in the problem. It is visible, so it takes no imagination at all. But the solution we seek is not visible at the start. It is no place to be seen, except in the consciousness of the person who desires it enough to change his or her mind. The trained mind heals. The mind accustomed to wandering out of control is victim to everything and anything.

MAKE GOOD THINGS COME NATURALLY

We want to use our minds first to create an idea of the thing desired and then to continue developing such ideas. We want to stay involved in the kind of thinking that keeps affirming, supporting, clarifying, and nurturing our great idea. We want to keep our creative thoughts going this way until our mind doesn't know any other way to go. We want to keep it going this way so that when we think about life, we think about it creatively. When we think about health, we want our minds to claim health for us and to rejoice in this claim.

As we develop this consciousness, the physical world will start to look like a different place to us. We will begin to see things in it, draw things from it, and realize things about it that we never knew or understood before. We will start to act in different ways toward problems and toward people. The world will start to react in different ways toward us. People that we previously misjudged will become meaningful to us. A lot of people who are essentially negative and troublesome will suddenly vanish from our lives because we're "no fun" anymore. And a lot of people more wonderful and helpful than we ever thought possible will come from out of nowhere. Sometimes they'll be people who were there all the time, but we just never noticed.

This whole outer transformation takes place very naturally. It overtakes us gradually as we go along. In other words, we will not have to run out and make it happen. It will happen as an easy and natural response to something that has happened within us.

How does it happen? No one knows! No one has ever known. Just as no one has ever known how an acorn becomes an oak. As with everything that comes through the creative process, the first part of it occurs in hiding. The infant has to be in the womb; the seed has to be in the soil. Much has to happen in secret before anything recognizable can occur. Sometimes we know how long it takes, as in pregnancy. We have names for the different stages of the inner process evolving. But we don't know *how* it happens. It is the power of life *within* us that does the work. We carry *within* us that which knows how to do everything. We must know we have that inner power and learn how to let it do its work without worrying about it too much. That is our part in the creative process.

WE WILL KNOW WHEN IT HAPPENS

We will never know *how* it happens, but we will certainly know *when* it happens. We will certainly know that it *did* happen. And once we understand our part in making it happen, we will change the way we live our lives. And we will be changed very much for the better.

Our real power is in knowing *how* to think. It is not just being able to think. We're always doing that automatically. But power is knowing how to direct our thoughts to produce the things that we want in our experience.

We begin to use our thoughts creatively when we develop a habit of implanting in our minds good, clear, persistent ideas of that which is desired. Then our deliberate and personal act of creation begins. And it begins at once. It continues as long as we keep nurturing it. When the idea of the thing is ready to show itself as the thing fulfilled, when the inner is so formed that in order to go on living it must become the outer, it will find a way to come into our lives. This happens just as surely as a chicken pops out of an egg when it can't live in the egg anymore.

When this begins to happen, at the very first sign things in our life are changing for the better, we need to turn from being totally involved in the creative aspect of living to the manufacturing aspect. Now is the time to take hold of ourselves, take hold of what is happening, and make some good judgments about what we're going to do about it. Now is the time to build upon what is happening and put it to proper use.

Remember, "creation" means made by God, made by pure intelligence, made by the action of Spirit. "Manufacture" means to make by hand, or by physical activity. The initial action in the creative process is always mental or spiritual, but the finishing action always involves hands-on activity. So, we first do the mental work and then sit back expectantly, waiting to respond intelligently when new things start to emerge in our lives.

GETTING ON WITH THE CREATIVE PROCESS

Perhaps we wish to have more money. Or we wish to have a better home or a new car. First, we create an image of what we desire in our minds. We do not bother with an exact physical description. What we need is an image that is very broad yet very clear.

Equally important is creating an image of ourselves as possessing it, enjoying it, using it, happily paying for it, and feeling worthy of it. We must paint ourselves into the picture. We do not want a beautiful picture with us on the outside looking in. So many people look at life that way. They know what value is, they know what good is, they know what beauty is. They have a clear picture of it all. They're like little children outside the candy store, nose pressed to the display window, wishing. We must always put ourselves in the picture. It is our picture, and we belong in it.

When the image of this wonderful home or whatever it is grows stronger and clearer, our minds will begin to lead us to act in ways that bring about our desires. Our minds will start to give us suggestions, directions, urges to do this, do that, perhaps to do something different than we've ever done before. Of course, this is where a lot of people hit a snag. We don't like to do anything we've never done before. We don't even like to go to a different place for lunch, or get up on the other side of the bed.

If we want to live creatively, we have to be flexible. We might get this kind of inner dialogue going: ''I ought to go to the bank and talk to the banker about this. *No, they don't want to talk with me.* Yeah, but I ought to go there and try. *No, I've had bad luck talking to bankers before.* Yeah, but I ought to go.'' Eventually, we will have to follow through because it is a necessary step in fulfilling our desire.

As another example, we might get the idea to take on a temporary job. ''Oh, I haven't got the energy. *Yes, I do.* No, I don't. *Yes, I do.* Where would I get the time?

I could use the time I waste sitting around pitying myself.
Don't be so smart-alecky.'' We may be moved to call
someone to inquire about such a possibility or just to
say hello. When we are working for change and our
mind offers us an opportunity to explore something
new, we must accept it. Because such urges often lead
to the realization of our dreams.

WE DON'T "MAKE IT HAPPEN"

It is foolish to think that we can know how to make
happen that which we're mentally working toward. If
we knew how to do that, we wouldn't be working in
consciousness. The reason we're doing the mental
work is that we don't know how to make it happen.
We need help from the wisdom within us that does
know how.

So, when the urge from within comes to examine, to
explore, to do something different, that which knows
how is telling us how. It is giving us our part of the job.
The creative phase is ending; the manufacturing phase
is trying to begin, and we are needed. Whatever it is
that comes to our minds is a sign for action. Our idea
needs help *now*; realization of it cannot occur without
us. Our lives cannot change unless we physically get
into the act.

REALIZING A ROMANTIC RELATIONSHIP

Perhaps we want to realize a wonderful romantic
relationship with a fine person. As I said before, we begin by creating an image of such a person and such a

relationship. We create, at the same time, a self-image of the kind of person who belongs in that relationship —one who has something to give, and who is able to bring something wonderful to the other person. Until we see ourselves as worthy, the only people we will draw into our lives are those who don't do very well and who aren't too choosy. So, we create an image of a truly interesting person, of what a really good relationship ought to be, and an image of ourselves as being able to operate successfully in that relationship.

What qualities should we look for? Any ones we want. What kind of relationship? Any kind we want. Don't ask around or look for permission. Don't model it after any other relationship. Make up your own mind and have it your way. You know what you want. Go for it.

If we remain focused on this image, nurturing it and elaborating upon it, getting involved with it, and spending some time each day with it, things start to happen. Things start demanding our attention and inviting our participation! We will meet new people or be given the opportunity to go somewhere or do something where there's a possibility of meeting new people. Even when self-doubt arises, we must go places where we can enter into new ways of thinking.

We may begin to see old aquaintances differently. We might find someone nearby who suddenly seems more interesting than we thought before. We may think of new ways to groom ourselves. You know, you do have to bait the hook. A lot of people have the bait but not the hook, so all they get is a bite and never the fish. The hook's the most important thing, but the bait must be very interesting. We might even think of interests to pursue that will make us more intriguing. These urges to make certain basic changes in the way we think and the things we do must be taken seriously. Going to new places, doing new things, and meeting new people are all part of the manufacturing process.

Some people in search of romance will say, ''I do all of that all the time, and it doesn't work for me. I go everywhere, do everything. I'm always ready for action, but nothing happens.'' They get no results because they haven't done the creative mental work first. There is no image within their consciousness generating great ideas and attracting great things to them. Without the mental work, all they are doing is sparked by mindless frustration. It's not coming out of enthusiasm over an idea created by their own definite work. They are trying to manufacture without first creating.

They are like builders working without an idea, a blueprint, or a plan. They are trying to build something without a concept, with just a load of building materials, hammered and slapped together. Something may get built that way. But you wouldn't want to live in it. No one else would either.

Many people build their relationships the same way. That is why their relationships aren't fit to live in. They are built poorly, because they are not based upon a healthy and desirable idea. These people have no idea what they want or of what they are getting into. And since they are operating without a concrete idea, they have no idea how to get out of it. As a result, they sit around and mope; they call their friends and relatives and whine. They struggle along with the relationship until something happens to force them out of it. And then their next adventure is no improvement because they haven't learned anything from the last one. They wind up in another relationship that has no foundation, held together only with hope and a prayer.

MENTAL HEALING FOR PHYSICAL DISEASE

The spiritual healing movement in this country got under way over a hundred years ago because of a desire to heal people who had been medically diagnosed as incurable or terminally ill. In the middle of the last century when medical science was largely undeveloped many good doctors carried little in their medical bag except a bottle of whiskey and a saw. That's an exaggeration, of course. But they certainly did not have the knowledge, the sophisticated equipment, the kinds of testing and treatment and medicines that are now available. So there were many illnesses that people were told they had to live with or die of.

The interest in mental or spiritual healing emerged from this background, and originated predominantly from sick people. These were people who had been abandoned by traditional medicine and who became determined to find a way back to health by some other means. Their religious background had convinced them that God could heal without medicine. These were very religious, very pious people who believed what the Good Book said.

By attempting to find out how to get God to heal them, they turned to their own traditional religions and made a shocking discovery. Their traditional religions did not believe they could be healed or should even try to be! Their religions admitted that God was able to heal, but as a matter of practice it was believed that God wouldn't heal unless, for example, you were a saint. These people knew they weren't saints, didn't know how to become saints, and weren't much interested in being saints. But they *were* interested in living and being healthy, whether or not the physicians or the clergy thought they should be.

These were not people who set out to undermine the tenets of organized religions or traditional medicine. They were people who were left in the lurch by both. So, although they may have been devout by nature, they were also bright enough not to let their devotion kill them by making them victims of the ignorance they were subjected to. They reached within themselves and out to each other. They began to examine the nature of God, and the meaning of life including their own lives in very different and unorthodox ways.

They concluded that God really was all good and created no evil, that life really was all good and that they were meant to live it in ease and happiness for as long as they wanted. They knew they had to die one day—they weren't trying to escape death—but they believed that while they lived, they were entitled to live in peace and dignity. So, they wanted to purge themselves of any belief that said this wasn't so. By learning to accomplish this task, they set the stage for what has come to be called the New Thought Movement.

ALL HEALING IS GOD HEALING

We use this type of healing concept to support every kind of legitimate, effective, promising, medical treatment available. We use it to support any other kind of treatment that is sensible and available. And we use it exclusively when there is no other form of effective treatment for us. We use it to support what is already known and what can already be done. But we use it ultimately to support ourselves when not enough is known and when what we want is what "they say" can't be done.

In other words, we do not use the practice of spiritual mind healing as an excuse for not going to the doctor or for not following the doctor's orders, if they make sense. We use it to help ourselves respond to sound medical treatment and to help ourselves when good medical treatment is not available. We use it because the creative intelligence, the healer, God, is everywhere, and is pouring into everyone's life as they become receptive to it. The wisdom of good medicine is the healing power of God. As such, it deserves our attention. So we never reject medical treatment unless it rejects us, unless it rejects the possibility of our recovery. If the doctor says, "This won't do you any good, but I'll give you a prescription for it anyhow," then don't fill that prescription! That would be illogical, expensive, and possibly dangerous.

WE NEVER HEAL DISEASE

We do not heal disease. We get rid of it by getting beyond it. Healing is about establishing health, not about destroying disease or anything else.

All mental healing begins with the establishment of a healthy idea in the consciousness of the individual, a healthy idea about the part of one's physical being that is now suffering from illness, a healthy idea about life in general, a healthy idea about one's life in particular, and one's body in general.

We immerse ourselves in such ideas by using our minds to implant them in our consciousness. We implant ideas that represent to us the healthy condition we wish to have created in our bodies in place of the unhealthy condition that now exists.

Therefore, the first thing we do is decide what we want to heal. Then we involve ourselves in a process of affirmation with respect to the rightness of our healing. We have to know it's the right thing to do. We have to construct an affirmation of total receptivity to our healing and complete faith in the possibility of this aim.

There are many techniques that will get us into this healing process. In fact, there are probably as many techniques as there are people who are pursuing it. However, there is no one formula that works better than any other formula, because the affirmation work that you do only has to make sense to you. It has to take hold of your wisdom and enthusiasm. Remember, we are not performing magical incantations. We are not praying to a distant deity asking for "his" help. When we do this type of healing work, we are directing our own consciousness to accept a healthy idea, to take it into its bosom, and to go about fulfilling it out of its own intelligence. So, the method that we use is whatever method we desire.

SPIRITUAL MIND TREATMENT

I cannot provide you with a sure-fire method, but I can give you a format to follow in designing one that will be personally useful. The format is what I call Spiritual Mind Treatment. Spiritual Mind Treatment is not merely prayer in the traditional sense. It is, one might say, scientific prayer. When I say scientific prayer, people look at me in a strange way because those two words don't usually go together. Scientific prayer is a way of reaching beyond human understanding. It does not ask for something we hope to get but affirms something that we know is true, that we claim for ourselves, and become receptive to experiencing. We call it scientific prayer because there is a definite way to do it, and we can definitely expect results to come out of it. There is no hoping and no pleading in scientific prayer. It's affirming a belief about something and expecting that belief to become our actual experience.

ASSUMING PERSONAL RESPONSIBILITY

We use Spiritual Mind Treatment to get the creative part of our healing going. Then we turn our attention back to life as it is now, whether we like it or not. We begin to pay closer attention to what our mind tells us about life as it exists now, whether we like *that* or not. We pay closer attention to the new ideas that come into our heads, the new information that comes our way, the new people who come along saying, doing, offering us new things. We let ourselves consider all these new possibilities openly. And we let ourselves be led into the kind of actions or decisions that seem promising—that may lead to something new or better.

This may mean any number of things. It may mean changing doctors or medicines. It may mean *listening* to our doctors and taking our medicine for a change. It may mean changing our personal habits. It may mean doing something about what we eat and how much, what we drink and how much, what we smoke and how much. It may mean exercising our bodies. It may mean changing our work or work habits. It may have something to do with changing our friends or relating to them in different ways. It may mean looking at our social values and our religious ideas and changing them. It may mean forgiving someone. It may mean all sorts of things.

But whatever it means in particular, in principle it always means the same thing. We must assume personal responsibility for the way we think, what we believe, the way we feel, how we express those feelings, the way we live, what we allow in our life, what we are taking in, and what we are giving out. This is *total personal responsibility*.

It may not be necessary to change it all, but we must assume personal responsibility for it all. Until we do that, we can't change anything. Sick people must make no one else responsible for their illnesses and no one else responsible for their recovery but themselves. It means that we don't sit around blaming our illness on society, our family, our work, our genes, a germ, the inefficiency of the medical profession, or the insensitivity of the government. It means placing the responsibility for our recovery on nobody but ourselves. We don't blame what the doctor knows or doesn't know, will do, can't do, or won't do. A sick person is in no condition to be evaluating the rest of the world. All energy, all attention, all mind should be focusing positively on oneself and one's healing.

To practice sincere spiritual mind treatment for your health and then to refuse or oppose sound medical treatment is to undo the spiritual mind treatment. You can affirm the goodness of health and the rightness of health all day long, but if, at the same time, you turn away from the things that can help you realize that health, you are contradicting the words of your own mouth. To practice effective spiritual mind treatment and then to involve yourself in medical quackery, religious fear or condemnation, or with people who think you are a hopeless case, is to undo your spiritual mind treatment. The soul is witness to the act as well as to the word; the intelligence within you that hears the word also observes the behavior. And the act always speaks louder than the word.

We must get to the point where what we do and permit to be done to us is consistent with what we say. Otherwise, we are working against ourselves. To do spiritual mind treatment and then lay around pleading for sympathy, using illness to manipulate people, acting less able than we really are, and making illness the focus of our life is to undo all effective spiritual mind treatment, also. This merely creates more confusion at the creative level of our consciousness.

SPIRITUAL MIND TREATMENT IS NOT MAGIC

Spiritual Mind Treatment is not magic. It won't work no matter what. It will work only if we work with it. When our minds start to get creative as a result of spiritual mind treatment, we must work to let that creativity, that power for good, those new ideas trying to emerge, lead us to involvement in life in ways that are consistent with the idea we have been affirming.

We call the result of effective spiritual mind treatment a "demonstration." When what we have created as an idea in mind comes to life as an actual experience in the physical world we have a demonstration. We have no demonstration until then. People ask, "How long must I do treatment work?" Until you have a demonstration! Until you have what you have been treating for!

Most demonstrations do not occur in a flash. I'm sorry to say that you're not likely to be doing treatment

one day and be swept up in a web of light infused by
unearthly music, and open your eyes and see the
woman or man of your dreams coming out of the mist
of time. Most demonstrations do not come into view
full-grown and finished. Our demonstrations usually
emerge. They come to life the way most things do, first
appearing in a very small way. With proper handling,
they bloom like tight little buds in the springtime. They
start small, fragile, barely noticeable. In fact, if you're
not looking for them, you're likely to overlook them
and pass them by. But if you do right by them, act
right toward them, they will grow big and strong and
very useful.

IT ALWAYS WORKS
THE WAY IT ALWAYS WORKS

People who are suffering from a serious, painful,
scary, life-threatening illness always have a great sense
of urgency about them. That urgency is part of the
pathology. That urgency we understand with compas-
sion, but still we know it as part of what's wrong with
them and part of what needs to be healed. It does not
change the way demonstrations occur. It does not
make the demonstration occur faster or more dramatically. When we do treatment work for health, part of
the work always revolves around peace and courage—
concepts that are needed to clear away the urgency
that so often causes people to think destructively and
do very foolish things.

Whether people have a sense of urgency or not, life
works the way it works. In the case of terribly ill peo-

ple with great panic, life still works for them only as well as it works for everyone else. It does not work any better or any quicker. Life is impressed by neither pain nor desperation. It heals us only in response to right use of our consciousness.

It is best to become committed to a life of self-healing while we are well. It is much easier to do effective spiritual mind treatment at that time than when our health is hanging by a thread and we can hardly think straight. This doesn't mean that treatment won't work if we wait until the last minute. But it does mean that it won't work any faster or surer than we can properly work with it.

Seriously ill people who are in the most need of the benefits of spiritual mind treatment are apt to reject it because it does not work instantly. They think that if the treatment is any good at all, it will work speedily. If it doesn't, they will reject it, sometimes bitterly.

People with this attitude are still being victimized by a common character defect that played a part in the formation of their illness—impatience, life-long impatience. It is part of the common stubbornness, resentment, resistance to life, lack of faith in life, and ignorance of the way life works. Life always works to heal, but it works the way it works. Not the way we wish it would. And not until we work with it correctly.

HEALING COMES AS FAST
AS WE CAN ACCEPT IT

Mental healing usually unfolds in our lives bit by bit, step by step, and this is usually the only way we are

able to accept it. If we know from the beginning that
a good demonstration occurs in its own time, in its
own way, then perhaps we will be spared the destruc-
tiveness of impatience. And perhaps we will be able to
speed it up by learning how to be very grateful for any
small improvement.

I often visit terribly ill people who are involved in
treatment work. I'll walk in and say, "How are you
doing?" And they'll say, "I'm doing better. Now I can
move my hands. But I can't move anything else."

"But you are able to move your hands," I will say,
"Isn't that wonderful." But they rarely think it's wonderful. They are usually disappointed. And their attitude affects their ongoing demonstration.

It is essential to focus on what we have, however little it may be. If we can't find a way to accept and
recognize and rejoice in any good that has come, our
healing will not move forward. It comes to us as we
can accept it. It slips away when we reject it.

If we know from the start what to expect, how to expect it, and what our part in it is, then we will be prepared to understand what a demonstration is. When
it comes, we will know how to receive it and how to
make it grow. That is, we will know how to move from
the creative mental work that got it started into the
manufacturing part that keeps it going.

It is important to joyfully accept and praise small im-
provements and subtle changes for the better. We
need to understand that every single one of them is
more than we had before and, therefore, a step in the
right direction.

HOW TO DO SPIRITUAL MIND TREATMENT

I can't show anyone *how* to do effective spiritual mind treatment, but I can advance a formula for doing it. Anyone can use this formula to guide one's thoughts in healing ways. I believe that the best approach for anyone is to take it exactly as I propose it until a more personal way is discovered. In cooking, we follow a recipe until we know how to make the stew. Then it's no longer one teaspoon of this and a half cup of this. It is now some of this, a bit of that, and it comes out just great!

The formula I use is a seven-step formula. Each of the steps is equal in importance because each step takes us somewhere. Each step means something in itself and lends to the integrity of the treatment. Taken together in a proper sequence, they form a logical and systematic stairway up to the heights of your subconscious mind and allow you to implant the healing idea that the treatment conveys. These steps are *Recognition, Unification, Affirmation, Denial, Re-affirmation, Praise,* and *Release*.

FIRST STEP—RECOGNITION

The first thing that we need to do as part of this process is to affirm that we recognize that the creative power of God, the power that heals all, is ever-present and ever-active throughout the universe, and is always making all things new. We have to recognize this power that we are going to work with and say something about the nature of what this power is and what it does. We do that in the step we call *"Recognition."* We could say, *"I know that there is only one God, one creative power, one creative purpose, now and always at work throughout the universe making all things new and good and perfect,"* or words to that effect.

Having affirmed that there is such a power and that it is doing this work, we quite logically want to become one with it. Because, if this activity is going on, we want to make ourselves part of it. Therefore, the next step is called *"Unification."*

SECOND STEP—UNIFICATION

We have recognized what the power is, how wonderful it is, and what it's doing. Now we unify with it by declaring something such as, *"This creative power is the sum and substance of my life. It now fills my mind and moves through my entire being, doing its good and perfect work."* If you want to get fancy you can add something like, *"I am thinking of God alone right now. Therefore, God alone is thinking right now of me and for me in totally creative ways."* Having unified with this power that heals, the next thing we want to do is direct it to do the kind of work within us that needs to be done.

THIRD STEP—AFFIRMATION

Next, we have to affirm what we want this power to do. Let us assume at this point that we are doing this treatment because we have a diseased heart. And if you have a diseased heart, the first thing you know is that you don't want one. Instead, you want a healthy heart. So, know what you want and treat for it.

Here is a model affirmation for a healthy heart: *"I affirm that this perfect creative intelligence, this knower of all wisdom, this doer of all good, now operates in all its power at the center of my heart."*

You have already said it is everywhere doing everything. Now is the time to specifically focus in thought. *"There it structures itself as new and perfect cells of every type, generates new and perfect heart tissue of every type, moves with ease to every chamber, every vessel, prospering my heart and my whole body in every way possible."* In this way you are affirming a much better idea than the one you held of a clogged and diseased heart.

So, we have affirmed what we want it to do and what we know about it. Now we come to a step that we call denial, and it's a very important step.

FOURTH STEP—DENIAL

We need to quickly and emphatically deny that there is any opposing power in the universe or anything in life that opposes this activity we are claiming for ourselves. We could say something such as, *"In light of the truth of the words I have just now spoken, I reject entirely any belief in heart disease as power, and I reject entirely any negative opinions of any kind about me, my heart, or my life. They have no power over me. They have no promise for me. They have no place in my thinking. God doesn't believe in them, and neither do I."* That's denial!

FIFTH STEP—RE-AFFIRMATION

Then you re-affirm, because *"I know God is really all there is, in me, around me, moving through me, and this includes my heart."* You affirm, you deny any belief in anything that blocks it, and then you re-affirm your original thesis.

SIXTH STEP—PRAISE

The next step is what we call *"Praise."* Praise is very, very important to human progress on every level because it generates positive emotion and enthusiasm, heightens interest and commitment, and makes us more involved in what we are praising.

You make people feel good when you praise them. *You* feel good when you get praised. But we're not praising God. God doesn't need our praise. God is perfect happiness and completion whether we acknowledge this is true or not.

The purpose of praise is to heighten *our* consciousness, not God's. It is to bring us up, not to bring God down. With praise, we rise up in consciousness to where the power is. This is a very important step in keeping treatment from becoming a morbid or boring process.

And it's very simple. *"I rejoice in this."* In what? In what you just said. *"I rejoice in this, my great and true understanding, and I praise the endless and loving creative power of God that now heals me in harmony with this treatment."*

SEVENTH STEP—RELEASE

Finally, we release the treatment. This step is absolutely necessary because it is the ultimate act of faith to release it and let it be so. This release illustrates to us that we believe the work we have done is sufficient, and that the power we have generated and directed in us is now doing the work. We announce to ourselves that we don't have to worry about it. We let it go; we release it.

The ultimate way to show trust in somebody is to let them go. For example, you're a parent with children. You want your children to grow up to have a sense of responsibility and be true to their word. You have to believe their word and let them go, and know that they are not going to get into too much of a mess. Now, your children could disappoint you, but God can't.

Another example: You're an employer. You want an employee to take over this department or that function. It will never happen as long as you're leaning over this person's shoulder. If the employee has any sense, he or she will quit after a while. And if this person doesn't quit, he or she will never get it right because of what you're doing.

We need to illustrate to ourselves that we believe in what we've done, so we release it. *"In perfect confidence I release this treatment knowing that the work is done. I turn to the business of the life before me knowing that within me there is an enormous healing now in process. And I let it be so."* That finishes the process of Spiritual Mind Treatment.

IF IT PERPLEXES YOU—

If this process seems too complicated, too perplexing, it's only because it's new to you. This is a simple and logical progress of thought from a point of desire to a point of faith. So, it if seems difficult to you, it's just because you're not used to thinking or affirming things that way.

It is no longer difficult for me because I'm used to it and do it all the time. But I had to stop thinking it was too complicated and time-consuming. I had to sit down with these steps and a sheet of paper in front of me and learn how to do work for myself. I followed these steps, imitating word for word what I had taken down in my notes because I wasn't yet comfortable enough to use words of my own. I know it worked for me. I suggest that you commit yourself to do the same.

Because if it works *at* all, it works *for* all.

Start by taking some time to decide what you really want to demonstrate. Get your mind off what's wrong, how awful it is, how sad it is, how terrible it is. Instead, concentrate on what you want instead of all that you don't want. You already have what you don't want. You don't need to treat for it.

GO IN THE OPPOSITE DIRECTION

Usually what you want is the exact opposite of what you have. Remember it's what you want, not what you hope for, not what you think you should want, nor what anyone else wants for you. It's what *you* want! Make it the best thing imaginable. To make it anything less is self-sabotage. You are dealing with an unlimited power, so don't place limits on it. It will make anything and can make anything, so why go for less than you really want? Furthermore, the bigger and better your expressed desire, the more interested *you* will get in it and the more likely you will continue to pursue it. A lot of people project such a tiny desire that it really isn't worth all their effort when they start thinking about it. They don't get what they want because they don't want enough. They can't stay interested in so little, so they get nothing. There is no such thing as too much of a good thing. As Mae West once said, ''Too much of a good thing is just wonderful.''

YOU CAN HAVE WHAT'S YOURS, NOT WHAT'S THEIRS

The only things you must rule out are things that belong to someone else. This includes their house, car, job, spouse, body, mind, soul, or their right to decide for themselves. This means that you can't do treatment to get them to do something you want, like marry you, divorce you, give you money, hire you, forgive you, or even like you. All treatment is self-knowing for the production of a self-realization. It has nothing to do with getting other people to do anything, not even with getting them to be healthy and live if they are not committed on their own to doing that.

We cannot do very effective spiritual mind treatment

for other people until we are able to do it for ourselves. So if this way of thinking is new to you, resist the temptation to use it to heal everyone in sight. That is a subtle delusion that helps you get off your own case too easily. This is a ''physician, heal thyself'' proposition. And this is why I'm not discussing in depth how to work with other people. There are professional practitioners who know how to do that. And there are classes and literature available in that area.

HOW TO GO ABOUT IT

The very first thing to do is give yourself 30 minutes, sit down, and write your statement of recognition. To make it easy on yourself, use my statement of recognition if you wish. Then you need a statement of unification. You can use the one I gave you word for word. Then you must get a little creative because the next thing needed is an affirmation. In other words, now you have to get into something that's particular to you and your desires. You see, there is only one God, one life, one being, no matter what you're treating for. And you are one with it, no matter what the treatment is for. But when you get to the affirmation, you have to decide what you want. Is it a bigger bank account? Is it a better love life? Is it a good job? Is it a good immune system? Only you know what those things mean to you. So, here is where you get personal.

When you are affirming what you want this power in you to do, be very definite but not specific. In other words, if you want a terrific job, using your greatest talents, yielding a good income, say that. Don't treat for a good haircut if what you want is a good job. But don't get into the business of saying, "It must be this job, with this company, at this pay rate." Trust consciousness to create the right job. There is more than one good job in this universe for you. Trust consciousness to know that. If you knew the best job for you, you'd already have it. But something in you does know, so affirm that it does and that it leads you to the job and the job to you.

If you are treating to heal a certain part of your body, say that. If you want to heal your hand, don't say anything about your ear. Be very clear about what it is, but don't get into particulars. Don't say what the doctor must do, what the doctor must say or what your lab tests must read.

Don't treat for what miracle medicine must be invented before you'll be able to get well. That's nonsense! When you do that you're not treating to implant a healing idea, you're trying to manipulate outer circumstances. You can't succeed at that. Trust consciousness to involve you in life in exactly the right way with whatever doctor it takes, with whatever treatment it takes, with whatever medicine it takes. Or trust life to lead you to other options. Life can do that, too.

The denial step must be tailored to your particular treatment, also. What you must deny is the power or the legitimacy of anything that frightens you, anything that says "no" to you, anything that stands between you and the good you wish to demonstrate. This may be a belief in competition, a fear of failure, a sense of unworthiness, a memory from the past, a belief in the power of odds, a frightening diagnosis, or an unpromising prognosis.

Know that a diagnosis describes a disease, but it doesn't describe you. A diagnosis is the nature of a disease, not *your* nature. And a prognosis describes what happened to somebody else, not what must happen to you. It reflects someone else's past experience with this situation. It does not dictate your future. You can't deny that there is meaning attached to a diagnosis and prognosis, but you can deny that these things have any power in your life.

Somebody who once came to me very, very sick, said to me, "I've been an unusual person all my life. I didn't fit in my family. I didn't fit in at school. I've always been a loner. I don't like the things other people like, and I don't do the things other people do. And now I've got this thing, and the doctor tells me there's an 80 percent chance that I'll die from it."

And I said, "Well, you should be a survivor. You've never done anything like anybody else so far. Why should you do it now? You're a 20 percenter if I ever saw one. Go for it. Don't get normal at this point." That's denial!

Your last real chore in building your personal treatment is the re-affirmation. Go back to your affirmation step and summarize; repeat it. That's all. And finally, when you've done that, add the step of praise, add the step of release, and you will have put together your first spiritual mind treatment. Now all you have to do is use it, regularly and passionately.

The trick is to use it in a way that compels your continued interest. You already have God's interest and commitment. Use it in a way that compels *yours* on an ongoing basis. Read it aloud to yourself twice a day only. That's all. You have to get away from the idea that you must do it all the time because that is implying that you don't trust the work enough to release it and let it be so. So, do it twice a day only, morning and evening.

I suggest that you read it to yourself strongly, clearly, and dramatically. If you want to, stand in front of a mirror while you're doing it. You are trying to implant this treatment into your consciousness. You are trying to make a deep impression in a subconscious mind that sops up drama. What do you remember most, some silly program on television or a Broadway blockbuster with power and action? Create high drama. And because we also tend to be impressed with persistence, do it twice a day at around the same time every day. Aloud. Dramatically. This is what makes an impression on consciousness, not episodic whispering or whimpering.

WHAT ELSE TO DO

After doing the treatment, go about your business watchfully. Look for new ideas, new information, new people, new opportunities. And when you see them, pursue them gently, but with interest. They may very well be the beginning of your demonstration. Or, they may be a waste of time. That's why you pursue them gently until you find out. They may be your answer, or they may be something that leads you to your answer. Sometimes we have to go through a long process of finding all the wrong answers first so we can get them out of the way. That's what kissing all those frogs is about. Any answer is a good answer if you call it what it is. When people interview for jobs, every job interview is a success. You find out that the employer either wants you or does not. If you discover that the employer is not interested then that knowledge releases you from that possibility, and you can move on and go someplace else.

Whenever you get worried, and you may indeed get doubtful and negative sometimes, stop right where you are and say to yourself, *"Look, the work is done. My work is not in vain. The demonstration of my good is now unfolding in my life, and nothing can oppose it. I will suffer this negativity no longer."* Then, do something. Do anything but mope. Go to bed, shine your shoes, run around the block, wash the car, just do something else. You will be surprised how quickly your mind releases anything if you turn your attention to something else.

Finally, there is no need to discuss your treatment work with anyone because it's nobody's business but your own. It is a private matter between you and God. Don't expose it to possible doubt or negative input from other people. Don't trivialize it by making ordinary conversation out of it. It's between you and God, and it is very important work.

To go any further with treatment for specific concerns, you will have to go out on your own. But here is a general treatment for the well-being of us all:

A SPIRITUAL MIND TREATMENT

''There is as much greatness, goodness, new-ness, and life in me as there is anywhere else, as there ever has been, as there ever will be because there is only one life, one God, one power, one presence throughout the universe. I am in this universe and am some part of it. So all that it is, I am. And all that it does is done through me. My new awareness adds to me, expands me, deepens me, enriches my consciousness with every kind of goodness. It clears my mind of all sorts of small, false, sectarian, judgmental ideas. It clears my heart of all kinds of fearful emotions. It causes a greater understanding to rise up in me, as well as a belief in myself, my God, my life, my world, and all of its people. I realize that there is no power in the past or in the things of the past, including my own past experiences because all the life there is fills the present and is the only stuff of which the future will be made. I praise, rejoice in, and am grate-ful for, my ability to say these words, to hear these words, to understand these words, and to let these words become power to me. And I declare, by action of this treatment, that I am profoundly enriched and changed for the better, and that as I go on from here, I go on with the creative goodness of God at work in me in new and better ways. I know and accept life as it must be lived, and I live it, knowing that all this is so. And so it is.''

PART FOUR

POWER—THE PRECEDENT

A number of years ago, Dr. Norman Vincent Peale inspired the general public with his "Power of Positive Thinking" philosophy. He became an eloquent and persuasive spokesperson for an affirmative approach to life that causes good things to happen to people, things that aren't necessarily supposed to happen in the everyday world. Among these things are physical healings that defy medical predictions, grand opportunities that no one dared hope for, forgiveness of what has been long-feared to be unforgivable, love flowing into the lives of the oft-considered unlovable, and money coming forth in amazing amounts from unexpected sources and to unlikely people.

Dr. Peale's work made an enormous contribution to the mental health of the general public in the second half of the twentieth century. However, this was not because he discovered the power of positive thinking, but because he introduced it to the general public in a convincing and inspiring way. His respectablilty as a main-line Protestant clergyperson speaking from the pulpit of the prestigious Marble Collegiate Church in New York City lent credibility to his ideas.

Since Dr. Peale's initial success, many other main-line clergypersons have accepted it and spread it further. Today, it is having an impact among many in

religious orthodoxy in the form of a movement far
from narrow theological construction, impractical mor-
alism, the image of God as a distant person, and
Heaven and Hell as places that one must end up. This
is a positive sign of growing mental health and
spiritual sensibility in religions that have long been
dysfunctional.

However, throughout history and long before Dr.
Peale began to popularize these ideas, many people
understood the power of positive thinking and lived
lives based upon that concept.

In America, the New Thought Movement, exemplified
by Religious Science, is founded upon the idea that positive thought must inevitably produce positive results.
Dr. Ernest Holmes, the founder of Religious Science,
devised a method of guided affirmative thought to be
used specifically to create and nurture a desirable idea
until it emerges as the desired experience.

The premise of this philosophy is that God is still the
Creator, but is seen as the Perfect Creative Intelligence
indwelling all the living and creating new life by action
of affirmative thought. This indwelling creative spirit
that we may call "God" is assumed to be all good and
all giving. This new concept of God is what calls for a
new way to pray, but it is neither a new idea about
God nor a new idea about prayer. It simply represents
a pure idea of God and a pure idea of prayer, unpol-
luted by theological contrivance and traditional superstition. It provides us with a God worth believing in
and exciting to deal with. And it leads to a method of
productive communication with our indwelling Creator that makes it possible to do the one thing that all

effective prayer requires—to pray, believing that it will be done, so that it can be done.

The authority for this type of understanding does not lie outside of the mainstream of spiritual philosophy, but right in the middle of it. It can be found by looking at ideas of God and prayer with new eyes, seeking a deeper understanding, and demanding a clearer and more practicable meaning, so that we can direct the creative action of God in our lives.

There is long precedent for this type of spiritual thinking. We do not have to abandon the wisdom of the past in order to create a better future. We simply have to bypass restrictive thinking and theological pretensions of the past, remembering that all such opinion was laid down for the purpose of organizing people into manageable systems. It was never devised to set people free to grow and heal and prosper as individuals.

In Part Four, we take a deeper look into three ancient and honorable "prayers" and find that each employs the power of positive thinking in creative action. These "prayers" have become sacred period pieces that are often recited ceremonially, but seldom taken to heart. However, they are inspiring examples of how wise people have always used the power of thought to draw the creative power of God as Intelligence within themselves into creative action in their lives.

The first of these is the prayer of Marcus Aurelius, pagan Emperor of Rome. It is taken from his immortal "Meditations." The second is the beloved 23rd Psalm from the Judeo-Christian *Old Testament*. And the third is the revered but often thoughtlessly recited "Lord's Prayer" from the Christian *New Testament*.

THE PRAYER OF MARCUS AURELIUS

Everything harmonizes with me
which is harmonius to thee, O Universe.

Nothing for me is too early or too late
which is in due time for thee.

Everything is fruit to me
which thy seasons bring, O Nature.

From thee are all things,
in thee are all things,
to thee are all things.

POWER THROUGH SURRENDER

The preceding prayer is the ultimate "Thy Will Be Done" type of prayer. It asks for nothing; it expects much. It makes no attempt to wheedle the Infinite with either pitiful pleas or hopeful promises, as if God were a vain tyrant in need of flattery. It is a prayer that expresses faith in the perfect goodness and wisdom of the Infinite and establishes a sense of personal dignity within the one doing the praying.

All this is necessary in effective prayer, whether we are praying for ourselves or another. When good comes into the world through our efforts, it cannot bypass our lives on its way to healing or blessing the life of another. This is why it is always useful to pray for the greater good of other people. No truly creative conversation with the Infinite can exclude us from its resolution. And no blessing can come to us that does not make us more of a blessing to the rest of the world.

This is also why it is wise to pray for the greater good of our enemies. Their greater good can never include our pain or destruction. The answer to such prayer must always include their triumph over ill-will and meanness and relieve them of the burden of enmity. Effective prayer for the greater good of our enemies may not, and usually will not, bind them to us in friendship, but it will always release them and us to more joyous and productive relationships.

Similarly, effective prayer for the greater good of our loved ones may not always draw them closer to us. In fact, their good may lie beyond us and ours beyond them. Our prayers may distance us from them and open the way for other relationships that bring us to our greater good. In other words, effective prayer compels nothing, surrenders every inclination to do so, and expects good for all.

If we believe that God is all—all-power, all-wisdom, all-love—we cannot sensibly approach God with instructions, with negotiations, with manipulation. If we are dealing with what we believe is Perfect Creative Intelligence, we must approach this power intelligently. We must bring to our creative conversations with the Infinite a belief that God has what we need and will provide it for us; that we are worthy to receive it, willing to accept it, and able to make something out of it— whatever it is and however it comes.

THE WILL OF GOD

The Will of God must always be for the greater good of all because life has never been and can never be in the least bit enhanced by anything less than that. The Will of God must always be devoted to creating our ongoing good because the Law of God, or the Law of Life, or the Law of Nature, if you prefer, is fundamentally a Law of Growth.

Therefore, the purpose of prayer is never to influence the Will of God, but to understand it clearly, trust it implicitly, accept it gladly, and resolve to do whatever intelligent and loving things must be done to bring our lives into harmony with it.

It is entirely counterproductive to say, ''God, if it is your will, let me recover from this illness.'' This does not honor the Will of God. It misunderstands it and so dishonors our lives. It casts a big question mark over whether or not we deserve to be healthy. Until we understand that God's Will is perfect health for all and that we are perfectly entitled to such health, we will not be fully receptive to getting well and staying well.

It is totally ineffective to say ''God, if you will give me more money, I will give some of it to the poor'' or ''to the church'' or simply, ''I will use it with more wisdom and love than before.'' Money doesn't come from God, and God doesn't care what we do with our money. Money comes from our sense of self-worth translated into wise action. Money comes more easily and more abundantly to those who know they are valuable to the world in which they live. Money grows and is good for those who like it, let themselves enjoy it, and handle it wisely.

So, the effective way to pray for money is to affirm its endless supply through the Universe, its goodness as a means of promoting happy living, our right to live abundantly, and our perpetual access to God's great wisdom concerning how to attract it, use it, and multiply it. This is the consciousness that brings us into harmony with the true Will of God where our wealth is concerned.

Anyone who prays this way persistently and with conviction will not only get more money but will also live better because of it. In addition, he or she will become a valuable asset to the general good and the economic health of the world.

It is all too common for pious people to blame the Will of God for their suffering. When they are lost and empty and cannot think of what to do, they try to comfort themselves by degrading the Will of God. They say that it is God's Will for them to be diseased, to have their mortgage foreclosed, their job abolished, or their car broken down.

Then they go on to say that there must be something to learn from it. But they are never sure just what that might be. What they need to learn is that the Will of God is always for a perfect life for all the living. The Will of God is for health, prosperity, love, and success.

Only when we understand the Will of God in this way can we pray effectively. Only then can we totally surrender to it, believing in the total wisdom of God, the perfect love of God, and God's ever-present power and everlasting willingness to let us have exactly as much good of any kind as we can accept for ourselves.

DON'T CHANGE GOD'S MIND— CHANGE YOURS

Therefore, the purpose of effective prayer of any kind is not to get God to do anything, but to "make ready the way of the Lord." This means to think of God correctly and to speak of God intelligently and, at the same time, to think and talk about ourselves correctly and intelligently.

Perfect Intelligence is a reflection of perfect love. Perfect love of the Infinite is absolute trust in its willingness to heal and bless our lives. Perfect love of self is the absolute conviction that we are entirely worthy in the "Mind of God" to receive the very best.

Effective prayer of any kind, following any formula, is a conversation between the individual and God. It continues until the person is convinced that God's Will is all good and is being done in his or her life in all things and, in particular, in what that person is praying for. When that conviction is established in the consciousness of the one doing the praying, the thing prayed for begins its transformation from desire to experience, from image to form, from seed to flower.

Let's take a closer look at the prayer of Marcus Aurelius:

"Everything harmonizes with me that is harmonious to thee, O Universe."

This affirmation clarifies something essential to the success of prayer. It says that my desire for perfection in my health, in my work, in my relationships, in whatever, must be the Will of God. If God is as we say we believe—all-wise, all-loving, all-giving, and all-forgiving—and if God is perfection, then only one conclusion may be drawn: *"What I want is all right with God. It is in perfect harmony with God's plan for a perfect world. There cannot be a perfect world while my life is imperfect. As I grow better, with God's power, not only do I make a better life for me but I also make a better world. There*

*is a perfectly good and natural way for my life to be healed,
blessed, and enriched. God is providing it. I am accepting it.
And it is happening in me, as me, and through me right
now.''*

**''Nothing for me is too early or too late, which is in
due time for thee.''**

It is very human to want what we want when we
want it. It is an infantile trait that is usually overcome
with maturity but that frequently re-emerges when we
become desperate enough to resort to prayer. Prayer
is not a way of life for most people. That is why most
people are so clumsy at it and so unbelieving in it. We
normally tend to pray when all else fails. We pray
when all hope is gone and when we have stopped expecting a good result. Therefore, we do not ''pray believing it shall be done'' as the Scriptures advise.
Instead, we pray, not believing that it will be done. We
pray, merely hoping that we will not suffer too much
or too long.

The more desperate we are for our answered prayer,
our demonstration, the less patience we have with the
process. We believe time is running out, and it will
soon be too late. We do not understand that it is never
too late for goodness to come to us. It is never too late
to start living more fully. We do not really understand
that there is no end to life and no limit to our opportunity. And we never will understand this until we begin to experience success in prayer.

When we pray effectively, our health begins to

return; our prosperity begins to flow; our success begins to take form; our general well-being begins to flourish. As we keep praying effectively and start living in harmony with our prayers, the demonstration of our good continues to unfold, expand, and become obvious in our experience.

Nothing happens as the result of effective prayer before we can handle it or after it is too late to do us any good. We must learn that the prayer is answered when it is uttered, and we must develop the gratitude and the courage to live from the prayer. We must live life as if the good we pray for is here right now, because it is. Our prayer is not to create goodness, but to make ourselves ready and able to recognize it and enjoy it.

Notice how often people pray for their good to come in the future. They are certain that they will be healthier in a few days or months. They are sure that they will have more money next year. They know that the right person will come along someday. But when we pray, we are dealing with a present Power. We are dealing with a Creative Power that knows only the present and is creating right now. Therefore, we must be ready to accept our good right now. We will never get better tomorrow unless we get better today.

And just as our good can never come too soon, it can never come too late. We can delay learning a correct way to let it happen, but when at last we do approach it correctly, its response to us is immediate.

In the Mind of God, the time is always now; the place is always here; and whoever we are, we are

God's perfect intention for a better and more fulfilling life of every imaginable kind.

"Everything is fruit to me that thy seasons bring, O Nature."

This affirmation states that no harm can ever come to us from God and that there is no terrible price we must pay for our good. It means that whatever must happen for us to have what we want can occur in a way that blesses all and harms no one.

It is important to be able to pray fearlessly if we are going to pray effectively. We should approach the Infinite in awe of the power we are dealing with but entirely without fear of what that power might do.

As we develop a consciousness that understands that God really is All-Good, we will be able to pray fearlessly and, therefore, more effectively.

"From thee are all things, in thee are all things, to thee are all things."

This is an excellent summary of the affirmations of Marcus Aurelius' ancient and noble prayer. It leaves us with a sense of peace and perfect expectancy, with a state of consciousness that compels the manifestations of our great desires.

THE HUMBLE EMPEROR

Marcus Aurelius was Emperor of Rome and de facto ruler of the whole world. Although he demanded much of the world, he surrendered all of himself to the Universal Creator.

It might be said that he could afford to approach God so fearlessly because of his immense wealth and power. However, those with the greatest wealth and power have the most to lose in life and the most to fear from the world. I think their abundant wealth and power comes as the result of a consciousness that is more in awe of God than afraid, and more concerned with making things right in the world than in reacting to all its wrongs. This is a consciousness of humility.

Humility has nothing to do with being less than we want to be. It has to do with recognition of who we really are and what life is really all about. Humility is accepting ourselves as more than our experiences. It is understanding our true greatness and knowing that it comes from a Universal Power that wants to succeed through us. Humility is accepting the challenge, doing the work, and sharing the good that comes from a surrender to this Universal Power.

As we devote ourselves to humility, we grow and flourish in all things. We become people in command of life in this world, starting with our own lives and then bringing good to all the relationships in our experience and to all the work that we commit ourselves to doing.

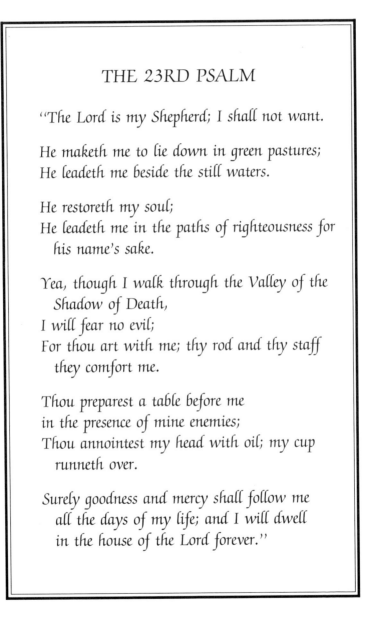

THE 23RD PSALM

"The Lord is my Shepherd; I shall not want.

He maketh me to lie down in green pastures;
He leadeth me beside the still waters.

He restoreth my soul;
He leadeth me in the paths of righteousness for
    his name's sake.

Yea, though I walk through the Valley of the
    Shadow of Death,
I will fear no evil;
For thou art with me; thy rod and thy staff
    they comfort me.

Thou preparest a table before me
in the presence of mine enemies;
Thou annointest my head with oil; my cup
    runneth over.

Surely goodness and mercy shall follow me
    all the days of my life; and I will dwell
    in the house of the Lord forever."

A SONG OF PRAISE

The *Old Testament* Psalms were songs of worship. Some were songs of lamentation and mourning. Others were songs of praise. The songs of praise always affirmed the greatness and givingness of God and the worthiness and gladness of the faithful. These songs are traditionally attributed to David, thought to have been an excellent musician and regarded as the most beloved character in the Bible, *Old Testament* and *New*.

He is not more revered by Christians than Jesus is, but he is more beloved. This is not because he was a saint. He most certainly was not, but he was a real life hero: remember what he did to Goliath. And he was a lover. He had a romantic disposition and a poetic nature. And when he went wrong, which was rather frequently, he humbled himself and asked forgiveness. This forgiveness was always given quickly because everybody really does love a lover, including the great and stern Jehovah of the *Old Testament*. And every-one knows that *"of him who loves much, much is forgiven."*

Whoever we are, whatever we have done or hold ourselves guilty of, we must approach the Infinite with love and praise. As we do, the Infinite responds in kind to this consciousness. For this is a consciousness that makes us more loving and, therefore, more lovable; more forgiving and, therefore, more forgivable; more compelling of good, and, therefore, more likely to be blessed with the good we seek.

We are told that we should pray believing. This

means believing not merely that God is and God can, but also that God will and God must respond. It also means to pray believing that our prayer can be effective and that we can learn to make it so. The first step is to approach God with words of love, of praise, and of expectation. As this becomes our habitual approach to God in prayer, our words will convince us of our sincerity and our worthiness.

Too many of us have been taught to pray with mere hope, a sense of duty, and a sense of unworthiness. It does no good to prove our worthiness to God if we don't believe in it ourselves. The Creative Intelligence we call God is a Perfect Intelligence having no ideas of unworthiness to overcome. And hope is not a creative idea. Hope allows us to survive until we can do better. But our greater good comes from what we believe in, not what we hope for.

WHAT PRAYER IS REALLY FOR

This brings us to the realization that the purpose of effective prayer is never to change *God's* mind. It is to change *our* mind. The mind of God always creates whatever our consciousness expects to receive. The quality of our belief or expectation is impacted by what we think about God and what we think about ourselves.

The purpose is to change the way we think, to lift us up to greater expectations for ourselves and about God. Love is the greatest uplifter; praise is the greatest way to express love. This is not a new idea. Marcus

Aurelius sensed it, and the 23rd Psalm, a song of love and praise, certainly reflects it. The orthodox approach to this lovely prayer is sweet but essentially depressing, which is why it is reserved for funerals or the walk from death row to the gallows.

What follows is an unorthodox approach. It makes this Psalm a living, loving God song to be expressed with purpose and power and to produce abundant good in the life of the one doing the praying.

"The Lord is my Shepherd; I shall not want."

The original Hebrew text did not say "the Lord." "The Lord" is a medieval European way of referring to the Infinite. This noble title humanizes the Creative Intelligence of the Universe for better understanding. And having humanized the God of all as a "him," they then gave "him" elevated status by making him not merely a lord, but the Lord of lords.

As orthodox religion evolved in the western world, we increasingly focused upon a diminishing God, by making "him" more manlike, rather than expanding all humankind by encouraging both men and women to rise up and be more Godlike. This is why most people pray to have God look down upon them or to come down among them to relieve their pain and turmoil. However, effective prayer does not bring God down into our troubles; it lifts us out. In order to get us clear out of our troubles, prayer has to take us further than the ideological lap of an imaginary king and lord. It must take us into a new realm of consciousness.

The *Old Testament* Hebrews did not think of God as a "Lord." They thought of God as a universal power that was the source of their lives and fortunes. They believed that this power saw them, heard them, spoke to them, guided them, protected them, and rewarded them. From the time of Moses, they understood that God was within them, not beyond them. They understood the importance of growing in personal wisdom and virtue because this was the way God cared for them—through the wisdom of their own thought and the justice of their own actions. They knew that there was something all-powerful inside them, and that they could rely on it. They said it was the great "I am" of their being. And they coined the word *Yaweh*, (in English, *Jehovah*) to describe the authority of God in them, as them, and through them. It means *"I am that which is."*

So, they would have said, "Yaweh is my Shepherd," meaning *"I am the guiding wisdom of my life. I carry within me the power to know better, to do better, to be better. I am filled with this Creative Power. I am enlightened by this Creative Wisdom. And this is why I shall not want. There is no need for me to look elsewhere for my greater good. There is nothing for me to wait for, to plead for. I do not need to ingratiate myself to some distant deity. I need merely to engage myself in a higher realization about myself and a deeper inquiry into the resources of my own consciousness, my own intelligence, my own thinking, feeling nature."*

The depiction of the Creative Power as Shepherd is picturesque and perfectly understandable. At the time of the Psalm, sheep-herding was a major industry. It was highly respectable and quite profitable. Shepherds were held in high esteem, just as ranchers came to be in the old American West. They were seen as figures of affluence, knowledge, and power. They were looked up to and relied upon to do what was right for the community.

In the case of the *Old Testament* shepherds, there is something else of significance: their need to be ever-vigilant. This special vigilance was required not merely to protect their flock from poachers, bad weather, and wild animals, but from the flock's own inbred stupidity.

Sheep are not very smart and not very industrious. They don't know how to find food; they must be led to it. They don't have any means of defending themselves. They have no sense of direction and wander aimlessly and stubbornly unless constantly directed. It is the duty of the shepherd to guide them gently and firmly because they do not respond constructively to fear or punishment any more than they do to sophisticated instruction. They really don't remember very well either. And the good shepherd never expects them to, but remains vigilant, patient, and always interested in keeping his flock safe and healthy.

In describing God as Shepherd, the Psalmist is, in a sense, describing people as sheep. The purpose is not to insult humankind, but to show how dear we are to God and how much we need the love and wisdom of God.

We must get away from the notion that because of our so-called stupidity, our wanderings from safety, our persistent mistakes, we are distanced from or rejected by God. Rather, God is the better side of our own nature, inseparable from us and permanently involved in bringing us back into balance, safety, and growth.

Just as the shepherd values the sheep and keeps them safe through the gift of his wisdom, what happens to you and me is important to God. God will see to it that there is a way for us to experience the best. A Perfect Intelligence must create only out of love and must, therefore, desire only the best for all that "he" creates.

"He maketh me to lie down in green pastures."

The meaning is clear and wonderful and extremely liberating.

"The Creative Intelligence within me has created me for a life of ease and abundance, or 'green pastures.' All that it takes to feed both my body and my soul is easily within my reach. I do not have to search on barren hillsides to find my good. I will never be condemned to live in a desert of poverty and limitation.

I am divinely intended to be easily fulfilled in all good things. Therefore, there must be a way for all that is good to come to me just as I am, right where I am. So rather than rush about frantically in search of my fulfillment, I stop right where I am and affirm the goodness of God and the rightness of my well-being and reach forward easily and joyfully for my good."

"He leadeth me beside the still waters."

Sheep are always hungry and thirsty, but they have little judgment when it comes to satisfying their appetites. They find food or water, stick their faces into it, and start chewing or slurping. If their appetites lead them into the territory of a stronger and less peaceful animal, or if they wander into poisonous growth, they tend to stand there and chew until they die, as they have neither the sense nor the speed to escape before real damage is done.

Sheep are known to drown easily because their ever-present thirst leads them into any stream that they find. They simply wander into the water and pay no attention whatsoever to how deep the water is or how fast the current. Their heavy absorbent wool can quickly weigh them down, allowing them to be carried off or pulled under with ease. One minute they are slurping away greedily and the next, they are drowning, without missing a slurp.

A good shepherd guards his flock against this type of hazard. In the quote above, the Psalmist realizes and affirms that he has within himself the wisdom to find still waters, so he may safely drink deeply of life without fear of being sucked under or carried away by unseen forces.

Many of us feel that in order to satisfy our thirst for life, we must place ourselves at risk of losing it where the waters run too fast. This comes out of a belief that we do not deserve to be filled and satisfied, that this good is not natural to us, that God opposes it. Instead

of letting wisdom guide us to safe and happy fullfill-
ment, we go the perilous way and live dangerously,
believing that this is what we must do to live well.

But the Psalmist knows better and affirms that the
wisdom and love of God within will safely guide us to
all the goodness of life.

"He restoreth my soul."

To restore is to fill when empty. It is to recharge,
replace, or renew. We all have times when we feel
empty, used up, or resourceless. We all have times
when life in the world seems to take everything out of
us and leave us feeling alone and afraid.

These are the times when we easily get into trouble
and make serious mistakes. This is when we look for
power where it is not. This is when we get involved
with people and things that take much more from us
than they are able to give us. This is when we bargain
away our integrity for what looks like something but
is really nothing.

Here the Psalmist sings a song of spiritual self-
sufficiency. He proclaims that the source of our re-
newal is within us and is everything it takes to put us
back in working order, fill our emptiness, and vitalize
our being.

"He leadeth me in the paths of righteousness for his name's sake."

This quote is a positive reminder that God is always
behind us. We have to get away from the spiritually in-
hibiting idea that God has no good reason to respond

affirmatively to our needs because of our "sins." What we learn here is that we don't have to get God to like us or approve of us before our prayers can be answered. We know that the right creative action of God takes place within us for no reason other than that is the way it is.

When we pray correctly, God as Creative Principle must respond to our prayer positively. This is what God as Creative Principle must do to be true to its own nature. The Creator must always empower its creation in support of a decision to grow and flourish. The universe holds back no good from anybody, but gives to all alike, simply because that is according to its exact nature. God does not know "our sin." Only *we* know "our sin," and we are the only ones who need to overcome it.

"Yea, though I walk through the Valley of the Shadow of Death, I shall fear no evil; for thou art with me."

This is the most famous passage from of the 23rd Psalm, and it is often used to promote morbid resignation rather than to instill a sense of power.

However, the Valley of the Shadow of Death does not describe hard, fearful, or painful times. Neither does it reflect terminal illness, nor the last walk of the convict to the electric chair.

This Psalm is a joyful song of spiritual realization, not a plaintive dirge. In this world, we are always living in the Valley of the Shadow of Death. We know very well that we shall one day die. The good news is, there is nothing to fear from death. The death that casts its shadow over this life is not an evil thing, and with this wisdom in our hearts we can live joyfully, going our way happily addressing what is, without the burden of a morbid fear of what must eventually come to pass.

The great mystics have always spoken of overcoming even death itself. They did not mean avoiding physical death. They meant healing ourselves of the fear of physical death so we could experience more abundant life.

Our ability to enjoy life and to achieve our objectives are directly influenced by our attitudes about death. If we fear death too much, we enjoy life too little, and we don't live it nearly as well as we could. As we learn to fear death less, we come to live life better and enjoy it more and more.

For many centuries, the great and wise peoples of all cultures have taught that each of us is alive because there is a God, a Creator by some description, who would have it so. It is as if God has given us a life and, at some point in our living of it, demands a death. If we believe that such a God is creative by nature, it is quite logical to assume that this death is not God's way of finishing us off, but a way of making something greater of us by taking us out of this world and into an experience that is not of this world. It is much easier to believe in a God that is never finished creating than in one who must destroy its own creation in order to continue being God.

As we grow in understanding of the total goodness

and presence of God as the eternal Creator of life, we realize that death is not evil. It is neither punishment for anything nor is it the end of us. It is a process through which we are moved on to a greater possibility. It is the beginning of a new phase of our lives.

Many people easily accept the idea that we have lived before. They can see that when we are born into this life, we die to another life although we do not remember that other life. However, we really don't need to remember it to live effectively in this one, even though that life must have been precious to us. Some part of us must have clung to it, just as some part of us clings to this life and does not want to let go. That part of us is not wrong, it is merely limited in vision. A crucial element in spiritual growth is the ability to expand our vision of life so we become more and more free of the fear of death. The way to expand this vision is to grow in our understanding of God as the Law of Life, the Substance of Life, and the Creative Intelligence in which the Universe and every form of life lives, moves, and has its being forever.

So, in this verse the Psalmist affirms that even though life can be fearsome and that there is danger in much that we do, possibly mortal danger, we can always find a way to live well anyway. We can come to the realization that all fear, even the fear of death, is merely a shadow with no power, no substance, and no reality. Shadows fade away as the light grows stronger. As the light of God in our minds and hearts burns bright, it dissolves all fear and lets us see things that were once invisible to us.

"Thy rod and thy staff, they comfort me."

The shepherd's rod, part of his standard equipment, is simply a stout stick that is for prodding sheep back into the fold and moving in the right direction. It is not a club, a whip, or any kind of instrument designed to inflict injury. But it has just enough clout to get the sheep's attention.

The staff of the shepherd is a long pole with a crook at the end of it. The crook is used to hook a sheep around the neck to pull it out of trouble when it has strayed too far from the shepherd.

In Christian tradition, bishops have always regarded themselves as spiritual shepherds assigned by God to care for a "flock." Although the bishops are dealing with human beings, not sheep, there has always been the tendency to consider their "flock" sheep who are not cognizant of their own good nature. There has also been a desire to keep them that way. For many centuries, most good people chose to resign themselves to the spiritual wisdom of others in true ovine fashion. So, the symbols of the bishops' office have traditionally been a rod, which has been transformed into something closer to a scepter, and a rather ornate staff, which is purely decorative.

The Psalmist realized that living correctly is not without its painful moments and that we all need to be prodded, pushed, and yanked back into line sometimes. He is also saying that God in us, as conscience, will always do that, no matter how much it irritates or embarrasses us. Now, this is not to harm us, but to comfort us; it is done to prod us to live correctly so that we may live comfortably.

"Thou preparest a table before me in the presence of mine enemies; thou annointest my head with oil; my cup runneth over."

As we grow spiritually, we come to understand that our only real enemies are ourselves. As Pogo, the comic strip character, sagely observed, *"I have met the enemy, and he is me."* This statement comes from a deep understanding of truth. The people and circumstances opposing our well-being do not come into our lives unbidden. They are attracted to us by our own inner negativity towards life. When we no longer compel their presence in this way, they will leave our experience. As we change within, so do all the circumstances of our outer lives. People, both friends and enemies, come to us because of what we are, not because of what they are. There will always be a place in this world for them to go and someone whom they really need to be with. If they are in our lives, it is because our consciousness demands their presence in order to show us who we really think we are and what we really expect our life to be.

Life is always showing us, in form, what we are showing it, in spirit. Show life a better spiritual you, and all the facts of your life will change to reflect it. Most people do not know this. They think that they can change their lives by struggling with the facts, the outer circumstances. They try to become happier by running off the "old" people and bringing in "new" people. But the people they bring in are not really different at all. They are just different examples of the same old thing. The enemy is forever within. And so is the hero!

The above verse announces the presence of the hero within: the personal Savior. The God power personal to every individual is recognized. It tells us that this healing presence is acting in our life right now, not waiting until the enemy within is vanquished. It is working for us in the presence of the enemy. The victor always appears before the enemy is vanquished and is the cause of the enemy's defeat, not the reward for it.

Our thoughts are often our enemies. It is common to think that we are not virtuous enough to have great things happen to us. We think that we are not able to live better, love better, or have more. These are hostile ideas. They become excuses for not improving our lot. Many people spend years working on their faults, overcoming their weaknesses, and suffering for their real or imagined sins. They believe that they must pay dearly to have these sins forgiven and purged. They can accept no great good until that happens, and yet they never seem to believe that it ever will. All this trauma amounts to nothing more than negotiating with evil. But evil will never flee while it stands a chance of winning.

The Psalmist tells us that all good is happening now. He says that the Creator instills good in the midst of all evil. The Creator does not go on hold until evil goes away. Evil has no power to delay the creation of good. Therefore, every good imaginable is laid before us right now with no regard whatsoever for our faults, fears, and failures. We can start to nourish ourselves with greater ideas and present ourselves with greater opportunities anytime we are ready. We don't have to become perfect before we can get better. Perfection is not the name of the game. The name of the game is growth. And right now, the Creative Power that is God is giving us everything it takes to let us grow. We don't get good by getting rid of bad. We get rid of bad by getting good and cherishing the good we get.

The annointing with oil concept follows through on this idea. In ancient times, the father indicated his heir; or the king, his successor; by publicly annointing the head of his favored son with oil. The entire family or tribe would assemble, including all rivals for the honor, all well-wishers, and all ill-wishers. Then the head of the family or the tribe, the supreme authority, would make it perfectly clear where the power was and would be.

"My cup runneth over" is a statement encompassing utter and complete gratitude. It expresses the realization that we need not ask for anything more. Proper and prosperous living and healthy growth have nothing to do with getting more, but has everything to do with doing better with what we have. In so doing, we make more. Our capacity for intelligent living is already established. Everything else must be earned by

learning how to do better and ever better with it. This is what is meant by, *"The gift is given."* Our cup runneth over, and we are left with the obligation to drink deeply from it.

"Surely goodness and mercy shall follow me all the days of my life; and I will dwell in the house of the Lord forever."

As evinced by this passage, the lovely and profound psalm gets deeper and richer verse by verse. If we converse with the Infinite sincerely and intelligently, we are bound to gain insight and certainty as we go along. God answers prayers in this way, by increasing our clarity, expanding our faith, and becoming more personal to us.

The Psalm begins by addressing the Infinite in the third person, "he": "He is my Shepherd; he maketh me, leadeth me, restoreth my soul." But in the fourth verse of the Psalm, the "he" is abandoned, and from there on, the Infinite is addressed intimately as "you." The Psalm begins by proclaiming the goodness of God. It moves on to address the presence of God as part of our being. Through this process, it becomes easier for us to believe in what we are saying and to expect results from what we are doing. Through effective prayer, we draw closer to God by action of the prayer itself.

In this final verse we come to understand why the Psalmist is certain that goodness and mercy shall follow him all the days of his life, and that he will forever be sheltered from the evils of the world.

When we talk about goodness in terms of God, it can mean only givingness. When we talk about God's mercy, it can mean only forgiveness. All the Infinite does for every person is to give endlessly and forgive eternally, no matter what.

It is a wonderful thing to come to the realization that we shall never be beyond the capacity or the disposition of God's great givingness. We cannot be separated from our greater possibility by age, sect, sin, or any other human factor. Nothing on earth can possibly get in the way of our spiritual growth, and nothing in Heaven wants to.

And finally, dwelling in the house of the Lord forever clarifies a very important thing: We are not created to make the world a good place; we are here to live well in the world as it is. The world is not a place; it is a consciousness. The world is people thinking; consequently, life is happening. We are these people, and we each have a part to play. We need to play it well, for as we do, the world is blessed. And so we find our happiness not in *solving* all the problems of the world, but in ceasing to be one of those problems.

"THE LORD'S PRAYER"

"Our Father which art in heaven, hallowed
  be thy name.

Thy kingdom come.
Thy will be done in earth, as it is in heaven.

Give us this day our daily bread.

And forgive us our trespasses
as we forgive those who trespass against us.

And lead us not into temptation,
but deliver us from evil."

THE PRAYER'S GREATEST SIGNIFICANCE

Many prayers have been written that encompass both beauty of language and simplicity of faith. But the prayer that we have come to call "The Lord's" is the only one that has endured in universal usage. It was first intoned in Latin and later made its way into just about all of the languages of the world.

Tradition says that the prayer came out of the lips of Jesus, who wanted to teach his followers how to pray. Whether it did or did not is of little importance; its value lies not in where it came from, but in what it has become.

Among Christians, it has become a universally accepted means of conversing with the Infinite. It has also become a unifying force, as it is the only prayer that has commonality among every Christian denomination. It has become an acceptable form of public prayer to many non-Christians, as well, and to many people who, although Christian by birth, have little professed interest in either religion or prayer.

This universal acceptability stems from the fact that this prayer is much more than a beautifully composed text; it is nonthreatening, nonjudgmental, and not insulting to one's basic intelligence, as well. It does not promote any restrictive theological concept or compel any exaggerated religiosity. In other words, there is nothing pompous or mysterious about it.

THE PRAYER'S GREATEST PROBLEM

The greatest problem with "The Lord's Prayer" is that it is always in danger of becoming meaningless cant and thereby delusionary. It makes people think that they accomplish much more than they actually do in pious recitation. This always reminds me of Hamlet's murderous king when he realizes his prayer for forgiveness is in vain: *"My words rise up, my thoughts remain below. Words without thoughts cannot to heaven go."*

Effective prayer depends upon impressive imaging in the mind of the one doing the praying. The Creative Power speaks no earthly language; it reads all human thought and responds to thought alone. It creates for us according to the images we construct in our consciousness. One excellent way of constructing favorable images that depict the quality of life we seek is through language and, in particular, through the words we say in prayer. But we must understand precisely what we are saying, pay close attention to it, and mean every word of it.

GOD DOESN'T SPEAK ENGLISH

God doesn't speak English or French or even Latin. The Infinite only responds to us by tuning in on our thoughts. Although thought may originate in any language, our images of thought have universal meaning. During effective prayer, we construct images of our desires and fill them with expectancy using whatever language we know. During effective prayer, we are never really talking to God. We are carrying on a dialogue with ourselves about God, the Creative Power, and what we want it to create. This prayerful dialogue elevates our thoughts to believe in the rightness of our desires. It creates affirmative, acceptable, and expectant images of our desires within the depths of our being. And the God within, the spirit of life itself, the father, mother, or generator of all life, reads our true hearts and moves within us to create our individual good. When our good comes to us, we call it something, in English. God calls it nothing. God simply knows it is God being God beyond all human description.

A DEEPER UNDERSTANDING IS NEEDED

We tend to recite "The Lord's Prayer" thoughtlessly. We do this when we race through it while alone, or stand up in church or any other assembly and rattle it off, hoping to appear appropriately pious. If we were to ask people who do this regularly what "The Lord's Prayer" means, we wouldn't get much of an answer. The truth is, they have no clear idea; they merely know that it's a "holy" prayer and therefore a good thing to say.

Many people have lost track of the idea that prayer is supposed to produce a definite result. It is supposed to create in our experience something very much like that which prayed for. Prayer is not a pious distraction from evil and limitation. It is supposed to heal, bless, and produce tangible results. If our prayer is not doing that for us, we are praying incorrectly, even if we are piously saying "The Lord's Prayer" in the "right" church, among "respectable" people.

This ancient prayer has a deeper meaning than we tend to acknowledge. It reflects an insight into the true nature of prayer and shows that some people have always known what others often need to understand.

"Our Father"

Oliver Wendell Holmes once said that his personal religion was summed up in these two words: *"Our Father."*

"Father" is a human title describing a role played in essential life-giving relationships. There must be one who provides freely whether we deserve it or not. In a human family, we call the person who ideally does this the father. Traditionally it is the duty of the father to be the everlasting provider, because the family was, supposedly, the father's idea to begin with. The family came forth from the seed of the father, and the children exist because of the desire and intent of the father.

In the ideal human family, the child does not have to make its case to the mother, because the mother already gives all and will always see to it that the child is cared for. The mother's power is already committed to the child. The father's power must always be invited. The father's attention must always be engaged.

In universal terms, there is only one God, one Creator, one Life-Giver. It operates on the universal level automatically and without invitation. It also operates within each one of us in the same way, guaranteeing fundamental life for all. Our blood knows how to circulate; our eyes know how to blink; our body knows how to grow. But each of us wants to grow into something special. We want to do more than just be. We want to beat the odds, overcome the limitations of our environment, and express our individuality beautifully. So, we need the Creative Power of Life, God, to provide for us in very specific ways.

To accomplish this feat, we move in gratitude from God as mother provider of basic life to father provider of ongoing opportunity. The father does not withhold our good. The father simply needs us to grow up so that we are able to decide for ourselves what is good for us. As we do that, God the Father will see to it that we go out in the big world and succeed.

The Father reference in "Our Father" does not refer to a male entity in the sky. It alerts us to the understanding that our originating power, the power we need to go on making a life, is our common source, the author of our being. We turn to this source as the child does to the father for his or her greater good.

We must also understand what it means to say "Our Father." It is important to realize that we are connecting with a limitless power, a power unlimited by time, space, or any sort of difficulty or complexity.

We do not ask "Their Father" for our good. If it is "Their Father," it cannot be a power for *us*. We cannot productively think of it as "My Father" either. If it is only "My Father," it must have other people's fathers to contend with, and I must be in competition with others for my good.

We very much need to understand that whatever has been done for anyone can be done for us, just as easily, just as certainly. We need to know that all good comes from one source, by action of one law, for the purpose of achieving one thing: the greater expression of God's perfect life among all the living.

Furthermore, when we acknowledge that there is only one God in which we all live, and move, and have our being, one God who knows us all in love and supplies us all in limitless generosity, we understand how we must think of one another. There can be no intolerance or grudging acceptance among people who really understand what they are saying when they say "Our Father."

The spiritually aware have always known better than to move against those whom God loves. Every great spiritual figure has taught brotherly love as an essential precursor to successful living. Not one of these persons ever assumed that we are all lovable in human terms; in fact, many of them realized that we can be quite unlovable creatures. But this is precisely why, for ultimate spiritual growth, we must turn to "Our Father."

"Which art in heaven"

The "which" is highly significant here. It does not say "who," suggesting person. It says "which," implying power.

Our theologians have done us a disservice by reducing the Infinite to a personal form, so they might explain "him" more easily. It has made God easier to explain, but more difficult to understand as we should, and to love as we must.

The truth is that God is not a person, but a power that creates for us by becoming personal to us. There is no man in the sky. There is only a creative intelligence in, as, and through all things.

Then why does this prayer say God is in Heaven? Because, as God is not a man, Heaven is not a place. It is not a geographic location. Heaven is a state of consciousness. Heaven is pure faith in the good. Heaven is a perfect clarity about how to think correctly, know rightly, and expect faithfully

Even though not one of us always lives in this "Heaven," all of us can go there through effective prayer. When we lift our consciousness, our minds and hearts in prayer, we are in total and direct communication with God, the Creative Power, and that Power goes to work for us according to our belief. We then come back down to earth and let the demonstration of our prayer follow us.

During effective prayer, God does not descend into the everyday traumas of our lives. Our consciousness must ascend into the realm of pure spirit, where there is no problem. In this Heaven of perfect being, we must affirm our good, claim the support of the power of God to make it so, and then descend back into life on earth and let it be so.

"Hallowed be thy name"

Most people know that "hallowed" means holy. More practically, it means whole, healthy, and complete. This phrase refers to the true nature of God. "Name" is not used here as a label, but to describe a nature or tendency. In this ancient prayer we learn that God's nature is wholeness.

This means that when we pray effectively, we are communicating with a creative power that can do it all. Therefore, it makes sense in our prayer to go for it all and not to pray for less than we really want, thinking we're more likely to get a little than a lot. I believe we often do not stick with our prayers because we tend to pray for so little that we cannot stay interested. We always need to pray for the best and the most we can imagine. Not to do so shortchanges us and indicates a limited faith in the power of God.

So, don't pray to become a little better when you want to become whole and strong and complete. Don't pray for a little money, when you really want to become a rich person. Don't pray for a Saturday night date when you really want a full, beautiful relationship.

We are dealing with a limitless power. Don't make it operate within limits.

Also, reject the concept that we need to give God instructions about how to create our good, or when, or under what conditions. God understands that much better than we do. Don't let either fear or pridefulness block or reduce your demonstration.

"Give us this day our daily bread."

This is not a request. It is an affirmation. To understand it properly, we need to put the word "you" in front. "You give us this day our daily bread." This is a truth we must never forget, for it lets us approach God with an attitude of gratitude that is essential to our faith.

In the midst of all of our wants and needs, our pain and suffering, our fears and frustrations, we must always remember to be grateful to God. Even in difficult times, we have all that we need to get through one more day. We have our daily bread.

We do not have to live by bread alone. But to live at all, we must have bread, and we must have it daily. Without it, we will spiritually starve and grow too weak to deal with life in this world.

People who do not pray are always in this weakened condition. They are struggling to survive, gaining only by coercion, not by growth; occupying, but not possessing. They are being more used up than useful, losing more than they are gaining. They are not thankful for their daily bread, so they are not likely to get much butter. Until our good is loved for what it is, it will never get much better. It takes love to make more out of less. It takes love to create something good. That is why it is said: *"God is love."*

An old saying states: *"Prayer changes things."* But the whole truth is that only prayer really changes anything for the better. Ordinary thought can produce only ordinary things. It is the consciousness raised up in faith to a greater possibility that creates all things new. Our ability to do this, even when things seem to be at their worst, is our daily bread, which is given to us freely every day. It always pays to be thankful for it.

"And forgive us our trespasses as we forgive those who trespass against us."

Here again, this is not a request but an affirmation.

We do not have to ask God, the Universal Power of Love, to forgive us. We must accept the forgiveness that is always being given. But we cannot accept what we cannot pass on. We cannot receive what we cannot give.

This is not a prayer for forgiveness. It is an acknowledgement of our need to forgive those who have offended us, so that we may be free of shame for all that we have done wrong. It is ridiculous for the unforgiving to expect justice in their own lives. They are living with a consciousness of injustice, and like must absolutely attract like. The biggest possible foolishness here is to believe that our hatred or ill wishes are justified; they never are. Many people have heard with pious terror: *"Vengeance is mine, saith the Lord."* It seems that none of us is invited to help God do whatever needs to be done to set straight whoever must be set straight in his or her relationship with God.

In this world, we get what is coming to us. This is

not what we think we deserve, but what God knows we really expect out of life. Because no one can expect more than he or she is putting into it, we must always be people who give. In many cases, the only thing we can give is forgiveness.

"And lead us not into temptation, but deliver us from evil."

Here is another affirmation phrased as a request. It decries the greatest "sin" of all, which happens to afflict the pious far more often than the profane. It is the sin of spiritual pride.

Through our great efforts to come into power in our lives, we do not want to become ego involved but spiritually uplifted. We do not want to be like the hypocrites of old who walked the streets beating their breasts and giving thanks that they were not like other men.

If we do this, we will not overcome evil, but we will find an excuse for it in our "special case." We will tend to think that we are most right when we are most wrong. And worst of all, we will have placed ourselves so high above all others that no one will be able to talk sense to us.

Our churches are full of such people. Much of theological life has been formulated by them, and many of them have given both God and religion a bad name. The clergy have often been the biggest offenders and the hardest to heal of them all.

So here is The Lord's Prayer restated:

THE LORD'S PRAYER RESTATED
AS A SPIRITUAL MIND TREATMENT

''There is only One God; One Giver of all life to all the living, giving perfect life to me now.

This Creative Power moves endlessly throughout the Universe making all things new, leaving nothing half-done, undone, or in need of doing.

Just as surely as I see this great and endless power for good at work anywhere around me, in the turning of the tides, the coming of the spring, the movement of the stars, It moves unseen throughout all life, establishing order, harmony, and purity everywhere.

I know that the Power of God in me this very day, right where I am, just as I am, gives me all that I need to live beautifully and productively.

I release from my belief and therefore dismiss from my mind all fearful thinking and ideas that would tell me otherwise, whether such ideas be hard on me, hard on any other person, or doubtful about the goodness of God. And I am therefore established in the love of all life and faith in God's creative power.

I accept my personal good in a spirit of complete humility, knowing it to be evidence not of my worthiness, but of God's great goodness. I give humble thanks for it, praise it, and let it be so.''

SUMMING IT ALL UP

Each of these ancient prayers is based in an understanding of the Creator as an ever-present giver of all things to all people in response to any person's receptivity to the good desired.

Each of these prayers recognizes God in this way, claims the good being sought in advance, and expresses ideas that affirm belief in a God who gives good. These prayers deny or exclude from belief any thought that would doubt it. Each of these prayers is a prayer of praise and total faith. The good nature and limitless power of the Creator is assumed and pronounced from beginning to end. Also, each of these prayers ends on a high note, with a sense of completion and a sense of happy expectation.

These ancient and enduring prayers have all this and more in common. They do not ask for anything; they announce something. They do not promise anything; they accept something. They do not wish for future good; they accept the good as present and active right now.

These prayers come from minds that do not conceive of God as withholding good for any reason whatsoever. Their idea of God is far greater than that of a medieval monarch dispensing favors to the deserving. Therefore, creative contact with the Infinite does not need to be in the form of a petition, and it does not need to include any promises of great deeds or good behavior to pay for the goodness desired. In fact, effective prayer is weakened by pleading or promising because these attitudes create doubt in our consciousness and thus limit our receptivity. And what we cannot conceive, we cannot experience. Such prayer places us under a needless spiritual handicap from the start.

Many people will acknowledge the logic of this, but will still not bring themselves to learn how to pray without pleas and promises. They will tell you that they have always prayed that way and are comfortable doing so. Then, of course, the question must be: "Are you praying to feel comfortable, or are you praying to get better results than you usually do?" If "better results" is the answer, it follows that a better approach to prayer should be cultivated, whether comfortable or not.

Spiritual maturity demands that we stop being more concerned with how we are feeling at the moment than in how we are thinking, speaking, and acting. All habits have their comforts, even bad habits. Every kind of change entails some discomfort, even changes for the better. If we wait until we simply feel like doing better, we never will. Right action causes our good, which includes "feeling better" or being "more comfortable." Better feelings always come as the result of greater ideas being put into action in our consciousness. They are part of the reward for doing something better than before.

It is spiritually incorrect to pray in "futurity," expecting to get better, have more, be happier tomorrow or next year or when the winter is over or when the kids go back to school or when a special medicine is discovered. When we pray correctly, we are not trying to get something after something else happens. We are trying to get clear and receptive right here and right now before anything else happens.

If all the creative power of God is present and active

right now, and if we are in need right now, why should we pray to have our need met at a future date? To do so places our prayer under a Law of Futurity and we become people who are always waiting for something better, but mostly settling for something far less. This is why most people learn to settle for less than they could get. In fact, they are happy when they can just avoid the worst since experience showed them long ago that it was too disappointing to expect the best.

When people begin to monitor their own praying, they discover that it is filled with futurity in both word and intent. A new way of thinking and speaking must be learned. Some people will claim that they don't have to worry about this new concept because ''God knows'' what they mean. I agree. God certainly does know what we mean all the time. But we are not talking about what God knows. Rather, we are talking about what we, the ones doing the praying, know. To pray effectively for our greater good, it is essential for us to know that it is possible to have it starting right here and now. If this is what we know or want to know, it is what we must clearly and carefully affirm when we pray. If we are too busy or too stubborn to take care to do this, we are doing sloppy prayer work that will produce sloppy results.

We are trained to be socially careful more than to be spiritually correct. That is why we take great care in what we say and how we say it. This is important, of course. It is, however, infinitely more important to take care how we think, how we talk to ourselves, and particularly, how we speak in prayer. This is what makes the real difference in what we shall have and what we shall become.

Purposeful living has been the theme of this book. Purposeful use of the creative power of our minds is what we have been talking about overall. But this purposeful thinking, in order to reach its full creative flower, must begin and end with clear, well-directed, and dynamic God-thought expressed in prayer.

From the very beginning, in every age and every culture, men and women living in every kind of society, under every kind of god, through every sort of human experience, have included those who lived well and were happy. If this were not so, there would be no human life on this planet today. Although these people must have been radically different in many, many ways, they also must have shared some common idea allowing for their ultimate success. I believe what they had in common was a commitment to purposeful living, fulfilled by learning to use the creative power of their minds with individual fervor and excellence in a truly prayerful way.

So, in conclusion, this book is for all people, of every race and faith, of every age and background, who are dedicated to applying their God-given creative powers to the ultimate purpose of living—love, happiness, and spiritual unity.

Make no mistake about it—this is a life-long endeavor, so may you lead a long and fruitful life as you seek your true purpose.

AFTERWORD

More than twenty years ago when I woke up and began looking for a new way to think so that I might create a better way to live there were few books directly addressing people like me in a clear, practical way. And they were not to be readily found in regular commercial bookstores. There were no audio cassettes of any kind available, and the very idea of video cassettes would have been preposterous. Of the few books available the ones most precious to me in those days included Jo Coudert's, *Advice From A Failure*, which I believe is now out of print, and Vernon Howard's classic, *The Mystic Path To Cosmic Power*, which I believe is still in print and worthy of wide attention still.

When I became a student of The Science Of Mind, I was introduced to a much wider field of reading in personal spiritual development by authors featured mainly in Religious Science and Unity bookstores. It was then I discovered the works of Emmett Fox, including his famous *Sermon On The Mount*, and books by Raymond Charles Barker, who became my teacher. Of the Barker books, four influenced me most greatly.

They are: *The Science Of Successful Living, You Are Invisible, Treat Yourself To Life* and *The Power of Decision*. All these are still in print.

It is wonderful to realize that just over two decades later all bookstores are carrying many authors and titles addressing the issues of personal spiritual growth with clarity and dynamic impact, and which help one and all find a practical way to do something with their own consciousness that causes them to be healed, blessed and prospered in many ways. Not only is there wide variety in bookstores, but in all the many more places where books and periodicals are sold to the public on the run. It is great to see the distinctive covers of Louise Hay's books and cassettes calling out to one and all from the shelves of airport newsstands all over the world. I wonder how many people passing through those airports, busy with their work and travels, but not all that happy with their lives get their first glimmer of a better way to think and a better way to live from such products as these.

I also wonder how many commuters who once spent their time in rush hour traffic cursing and fuming at the delays and each other, now are enriched during that time because of the many spiritual growth audio cassettes that are now so widely available.

All of this is just great. And I am glad to be able to make my contribution to all that is now available for people today who are looking as avidly for a message that would make a difference just as I did all those years ago.

However it is important for one and all to realize that all these good books and cassettes will do no more for us than inspire and direct us in pursuit of our objective. So it is important for every person to understand that sooner or later, and I believe the sooner the better, he or she must commit to a daily program of spiritual practice designed to put mind in spiritual focus and heart in a state of fearless receptivity to new ways of dealing with old things. We must become committed to more than reading, listening and viewing the presentation of great ideas. We must grow even more committed to figuring out just what they mean to us as the individuals we are, and how to use them to make of ourselves the persons we want to be.

—J. Kennedy Shultz

OTHER ITEMS AVAILABLE BY
J. KENNEDY SHULTZ

From *RSI Tape Order Department, P.O. Box 2162 Spokane, WA 92210-2152*, Phone (509) 624-7000

Double Cassette Albums

#1 POWER THE PRINCIPLE		$18.95
#2 POWER THE PRODUCT		$18.95
#3 POWER THE PRACTICE		$18.95
All Three Albums for		$52.00

From *ACRS Tape and Book Order Department, 52 Executive Park South, Atlanta, GA 30329*, Phone (404) 636-4567

A LEGACY OF TRUTH, Great Minds
That Made Great Lives.
Paperback, 134 pgs. $ 9.95

GAY AND GOD, You Don't Have To
Give Up God To Be Gay Or Lesbian.
2 Audio Cassettes In Album. $15.00

**RICHER LIVING THROUGH WISDOM
AND COURAGE**, Get Rich In Heart and
Mind First.
2 Audio Cassettes In Album. $15.00

HEAL YOUR SELF ESTEEM, By
Recovering From Addictive Thinking.
2 Audio Cassettes In Album. $15.00

YOU ARE TOO MUCH, For All
The Trouble You Are Having.
4 Audio Cassettes In Album. $15.00